my revision notes

AQA GCSE (9-1)

DESIGN AND TECHNOLOGY: TIMBERS, METALS AND POLYMERS

Ian Fawcett

Debbie Tranter

Pauline Treuherz

HODDER
EDUCATION
AN HACHETTE UK COMPANY

The Publishers would like to thank the following for permission to reproduce copyright material: p.1 © Stephan Goerlich/imageBROKER / Alamy Stock Photo; p.3 © Stephen VanHorn/Shutterstock.com; p.4 © sportpoint/stock.adobe.com; p.11 *m* © Evgenii Zadiraka/123 RF, *b* © Will Thomass/Shutterstock.com; p.28 © Justin Kase z12z/Alamy Stock Photo; p.31 ©Ian Fawcett; p.32 © Dreamsquare/Shutterstock. com; p.35 © JG Photography/Alamy Stock Photo; p.38 *t* © TFoxFoto/Shutterstock.com, *b* © Kuligssen/Alamy Stock Photo; p.39 *t* © Lukas/ stock.adobe.com, *m* © Lukasz Engel / Alamy Stock Photo, *b* © AlexImx/stock.adobe.com; p.40 © samum/123 RF; p.41 © Polydeuces/ Shutterstock.com; p.42 © Pixelrobot/stock.adobe.com; p.45 ©Ian Fawcett; p.46 © Hoda Bogdan/stock.adobe.com; p.47 ©Dan Hughes; p.48 © Dinga/Shutterstock.com, *b* © Gl0ck33/123 RF; p.49 © Helen Sessions/Alamy Stock Photo; p.51 *t* © Bluefern/stock.adobe.com, *b* © Stringer/Russia/Reuters/Alamy Stock Photo; p.54 *t* © Digital Genetics/Shutterstock.com, *tm* © Unkas Photo/Shutterstock.com, *ml* © Coprid/Shutterstock.com, *mr* © Achim Prill/123 RF, *bl* © Guy J. Sagi/Shutterstock.com, *br* © Zoonar/Alexander Strela/Alamy Stock Photo; p.56 *t* © C R Clarke & Co(UK); *m* © Midosemsem/123RF; p.63 © Forest Stewardship Council® - FSC® - www.fsc.org; p.64 © Fairtrade Foundation (http://www.fairtrade.org.uk/); p.65 *t* © Juergen Hanel/Alamy Stock Photo, *b* © James Mann / Alamy Stock Photo; p.66 *t* © Michael DeFreitas/ robertharding / Alamy Stock Photo, *m* © DACS 2017/© Picture Partners / Alamy Stock Photo; p.67 © Hermes Images/ AGF Srl / Alamy Stock Photo; p.68 © Science & Society Picture Library/SSPL/Getty Images; p.70 © leonart /12RF; p.73 *b* © Juliane Berger/ Ingram Publishing / Alamy Stock Vector; p.78 © Holger Burmeister/Alamy Stock Photo; p.79 © sebastien bonaime / Alamy Stock Photo; p.80 © Ftfoxfoto/stock.adobe.com; p.84 © oYOo/Shutterstock.com; p.85 © Mbongo/stock.adobe.com; p.86 © LJSphotography / Alamy Stock Photo; p.87 ©Dan Hughes; p.91 © Photobalance/stock.adobe.com

The authors and publishers would also like to thank the following schools and students for the examples of their student work: Abingdon School in Abingdon; Ripley St Thomas CE Academy in Lancaster; West Island School in Hong Kong; Oasis Academy, St Joseph's; Bedford Modern School in Bedford; Highgate School in London; Nonsuch High School for Girls in Surrey and Cameron Farquar at St George's School, Harpenden.

Every effort has been made to trace all copyright holders, but if any have been inadvertently overlooked, the Publishers will be pleased to make the necessary arrangements at the first opportunity.

Although every effort has been made to ensure that website addresses are correct at time of going to press, Hodder Education cannot be held responsible for the content of any website mentioned in this book. It is sometimes possible to find a relocated web page by typing in the address of the home page for a website in the URL window of your browser.

Hachette UK's policy is to use papers that are natural, renewable and recyclable products and made from wood grown in sustainable forests. The logging and manufacturing processes are expected to conform to the environmental regulations of the country of origin.

Orders:
please contact Bookpoint Ltd, 130 Park Drive, Milton Park, Abingdon, Oxon OX14 4SE.
Telephone: (44) 01235 827720.
Fax: (44) 01235 400401.
Email education@bookpoint.co.uk
Lines are open from 9 a.m. to 5 p.m., Monday to Saturday, with a 24-hour message answering service. You can also order through our website: www.hoddereducation.co.uk

© Ian Fawcett, Debbie Tranter and Pauline Treuherz, 2018

ISBN 978-1-5104-3233-8

First published in 2018 by
Hodder Education,
An Hachette UK Company
Carmelite House
50 Victoria Embankment
London EC4Y 0DZ
www.hoddereducation.co.uk
Impression number   10 9 8 7 6 5 4 3 2
Year   2022   2021   2020   2019

Cover photo ©ILYA AKINSHIN - stock.adobe.com

Typeset in India.

Printed in India.

A catalogue record for this title is available from the British Library.

Get the most from this book

Everyone has to decide their own revision strategy, but it is essential to review your work, learn key facts and test your understanding. These Revision Notes will help you to do that in a planned way, topic by topic. You can check your progress by ticking off each section as you revise.

Tick to track your progress

Use the revision planner on pages iv to viii to plan your revision, topic by topic. Tick each box when you have:

- revised and understood a topic
- tested yourself
- practised the exam questions and gone online to check your answers and complete the quick quizzes.

You can also keep track of your revision by ticking off each topic heading in the book. You may find it helpful to add your own notes as you work through each topic.

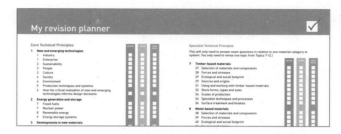

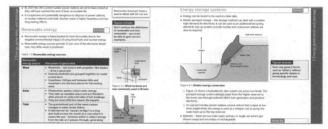

Features to help you succeed

Exam tips

Expert tips are given throughout the book to help you polish your exam technique in order to maximise your chances in the exam.

Typical mistakes

The authors identify the typical mistakes candidates make and explain how you can avoid them.

Now test yourself

These short, knowledge-based questions provide the first step in testing your learning. Answers are at the back of the book.

Key words

Key words from the specification are highlighted in bold throughout the book.

Exam practice

Practice exam questions are provided at the end of each section. Use them to consolidate your revision and practise your exam skills.

Online

Go online to check your answers to the exam questions and try out the extra quick quizzes at **www.hoddereducation.co.uk/myrevisionnotes**

My revision planner

Exam practice answers at **www.hoddereducation.co.uk/6 myrevisionnotesdownloads**

Specialist Technical Principles

(You will only need to answer exam questions in relation to one material category or system. You only need to revise one topic from Topics 7-9.)

Exam practice

Designing and Making Principles

(You should revise all of topics 10–15, but you may wish to focus on one topic only from topics 16–18, as you only need to answer exam questions on this content in relation to one material category or system.)

REVISED TESTED EXAM READY

Exam practice

Success in the examination

Sample examination questions

Glossary

**Now test yourself answers, exam practice answers
and quick quizzes at www.hoddereducation.co.uk/myrevisionnotes**

1 New and emerging technologies

New technologies change the way we live. They can have an impact on how we communicate, live and work, and how we manufacture and use products.

Industry

REVISED

- Before the Industrial Revolution, most people worked in farming communities, in small workshops or at home. The development of steam-powered technology meant products could be produced faster and more cheaply in factories. Many people moved to towns and cities to work in these factories.
- Modern factories are usually large warehouses located near transport links that contain manufacturing machinery used for **assembly-line production**.
- Developments in computers and processors that can control machines (**computer numerically controlled** or CNC machines) have led to increasing **automation** of repetitive tasks.
- **Robotics** are now used extensively in many industries. Robot arms can perform many tasks on a production line with precision and speed, replacing human operators.

> **Assembly-line production**: a series of workers and machines in a factory who progressively assemble identical items.
>
> **Computer numerically controlled (CNC)**: automated machines which are operated by computers.
>
> **Automation**: the use of automatic equipment in manufacturing.
>
> **Robotics**: technology involved in the design, building, operation and use of robots.
>
> **Innovation**: inventing and developing ideas into products.

Figure 1.1 Robot arms are now used in many industries, including the car industry

- Developments in communication technology have also changed where and how we work.
- The internet and mobile technology (particularly broadband and wifi) mean we can now communicate quickly and easily with people at anytime and anywhere. We can work remotely, and with people based in different places all around the world.

Enterprise

REVISED

- Businesses and entrepreneurs look for gaps in the market and aim to develop creative new ideas, invent new products and bring them to market.
- **Innovation** is often made possible by new and emerging technologies. These technologies can allow existing products or processes to be improved, or products and processes be developed in a completely new way.

- **Crowdfunding** is a method of raising money for a project by getting lots of people to give small amounts of money. It has been made possible by the development of the internet and social media.
- Many retailers now sell their products online. This is called **virtual retailing**.
- Retailers also make use of **virtual marketing**. This uses websites, social media and email to market a product and increase brand awareness.
- Tech **co-operatives** have also been made possible by new technologies. These are worker-owned businesses that provide technical support and consulting to other companies with communications and computer technology goods and services.
- Social media and the internet have allowed people to connect directly with producers of products and have increased awareness of fair trade. The **fair trade** movement aims to achieve fair and improved trading conditions for producers in developing countries and to promote sustainability.

Sustainability

REVISED ☐

- Product manufacture uses a huge number of resources. Processing raw materials and converting them into products consumes huge amounts of energy.
- **Sustainability** is about meeting our own present-day needs without compromising the needs of future generations. New technologies can be used to help us manufacture products more sustainably.
- **Finite resources** are those that do not renew themselves quickly. Their use is not sustainable and therefore should be limited.
- **Non-finite resources** can be replenished quickly and are therefore more sustainable than finite resources.

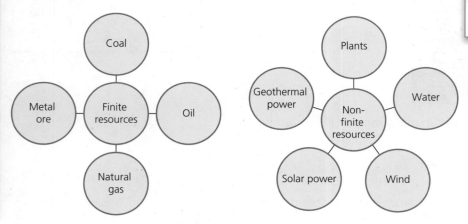

Figure 1.2 New technologies have helped us to make use of more sustainable non-finite resources

- At the end of a product's life its disposal can have an impact on the environment. Landfill can cause pollution, damage animal habitats and create noise and destruction. New technologies are helping to develop alternatives to landfill and developments in materials and recycling technology mean more products can now be recycled at the end of their life.

Crowdfunding: a method of funding a project by raising money from large numbers of people using the internet.

Virtual marketing: marketing techniques that get websites, social networks or their users to pass on marketing messages to other websites and users to increase brand awareness.

Virtual retailing: selling products on the internet.

Co-operative: a business owned, governed and self-managed by its workers.

Fair trade: a movement that aims to achieve fair and better trading conditions and opportunities that promote sustainability for developing countries.

Sustainability: designing to maintain the environment today and in the future.

Finite resource: a resource that will run out.

Non-finite resource: a resource that if managed properly will not run out.

Exam practice answers at **www.hoddereducation.co.uk/6 myrevisionnotesdownloads**

People

- Designers create new products because of customer need or because of developments in technology.
- **Technology push** is where new technologies or materials are developed, leading to designers developing new products that use them. The Apple iPad is an example of technology push (people didn't know they wanted it until it was launched).
- **Market pull** is where users want an existing product to be improved or redeveloped to meet their needs. Market research is carried out to identify how existing products can be improved to meet those needs. For example, BMW redeveloped the iconic Mini car of the 1950s to meet the needs of modern car users.
- Developments in technology have caused some jobs to disappear. Automation and robotics on production lines have replaced factory workers in some cases (although new jobs have been created in designing, manufacturing, programming and maintaining machinery).
- Some traditional job roles still exist, but new technologies have changed the way tasks are performed. For example, designers now often use CAD (computer aided design) software rather than hand-drawn designs; people use computers and email to communicate rather than typewriters and letters.

> **Technology push:** where new technologies or materials are developed and designers develop new products that use them.
>
> **Market pull:** where users want an existing product to be improved or redeveloped to meet their needs.
>
> **Culture:** the values, beliefs, customs and behaviours of groups of people and societies.

Culture

- **Culture** means the values, beliefs, customs and behaviours of groups of people and societies.
- Fashions and trends often influence the design of products. These can be influenced by different groups of people (for example, musicians, film stars or celebrities) and are often driven by the challenge to keep up with the latest technology.
- It is important for designers to understand and respect the views and beliefs of different cultures, including those of different faiths and with different religious beliefs, when designing products.

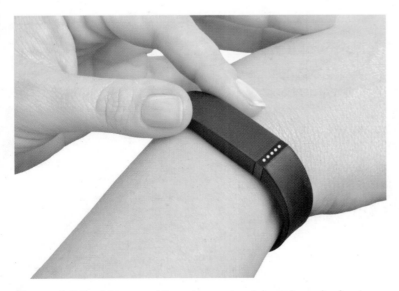

Figure 1.3 Fashions and trends can be driven by a desire to keep up with the latest technology

Society

- Designers have a responsibility to design products that meet the needs of everyone in society. They must take into account that different groups (for example, disabled or elderly people, or different religious groups) have different needs.
- Developments in technology have led to the emergence of products that help those with a disability to carry out everyday activities. For example, 3D printing and bio-electronics are helping to produce prosthetics to replace missing limbs and give disabled people extra functionality.
- New technologies have also allowed designers to consider the needs of the elderly. Products include: smartphones designed specifically for the elderly with simplified interfaces, larger buttons and screens, detachable keypads, hearing aid compatibility and louder speakers.
- Different faiths may interpret colours, symbols, shapes and ideas differently, and an awareness of these can contribute to the success of a product.

Figure 1.4 Developments in technology have helped those with a disability to carry out a range of activities

Environment

Continuous improvement and efficient working

- Designers can use new technologies to continually improve their products and working practices, making them more efficient and improving their performance.
- Continuous improvement can save time and make use of fewer resources, reducing costs and environmental impact.
- The increased efficiency of products can be positive for the environment. For example, if an electrically-powered product is made more efficient, it will use less energy and therefore put less pressure on non-finite resources. Using less material in a product can have a similarly positive impact.
- Efficient working processes can also be beneficial for the environment. Efficient, automated production lines can produce products very quickly. Computer-controlled machines and robots are very precise, leading to fewer errors and less waste.

Pollution and global warming

- Producing new products uses up valuable resources such as oil, metal ores and timber.
- Converting raw materials into products uses energy, which if produced by burning fossil fuels releases pollutants including smoke, sulphur dioxide, carbon monoxide and carbon dioxide (CO_2).
- CO_2 is a greenhouse gas that contributes to **global warming**.
- Technology that uses alternative energy sources such as the sea, wind, sun and rivers can help to minimise the impact of products on the environment.

Production techniques and systems

- Most production lines are now automated and make use of CNC machines that allow products to be made quickly and accurately.
- **Computer-aided design (CAD)** allows designers to design and model on screen. Designs can be manipulated and adapted easily and shared from anywhere in the world.
- **Computer-aided manufacture (CAM)** allows CAD designs to be produced. It is faster and more efficient than traditional manufacturing methods. Using CAM also increases precision as well as efficiency and speed.
- **Flexible manufacturing systems (FMS)** organise production into cells of CNC machines, with each cell performing a different task. FMS are very flexible – they can be set up to produce new products quickly and easily.
- **Just in time (JIT) production** is a production method that means materials arrive at a factory just in time for production.
- JIT allows for **lean manufacturing**, which focuses on reducing waste.

Global warming: an increase in the temperature of the Earth's atmosphere due to higher levels of CO_2.

Computer-aided design (CAD): design work created on computer software packages which can control CAM machines.

Computer-aided manufacture (CAM): machines which manufacture products, controlled by computers.

Flexible manufacturing system (FMS): flexibility in a system which allows it to react to predicted or unpredicted changes during manufacturing.

Just in time (JIT) production: reduces flow time within production as items needed are delivered just in time for the assembly of the product.

Lean manufacturing: focusing on reduction of waste when manufacturing.

How the critical evaluation of new and emerging technologies informs design decisions

- Planned obsolescence – this is when a manufacturer designs a product to have a shorter lifespan.
- Products become **obsolete** or unfashionable or just stop functioning as efficiently – this allows manufacturers to bring out a new version of the product and keep sales at a steady level.
- This creates waste as products are thrown away and so impacts on the environment.
- Design for maintenance – performing functions on a product to help keep it working correctly throughout its life.
- Some products are made up of modules which can be repaired and replaced, rather than the whole product having to be replaced. Modules also allow for parts of the product (like a PC) to be upgraded.
- **Ethics** – to keep prices low, companies cut costs in a variety of ways.
- Automated factories lower workforce costs, but people are forced out of their jobs.
- Using countries with cheap labour reduces costs, but working conditions are invariably poor.
- The environment – manufacturing a product uses **raw materials** and energy which impact on the environment.
- Designers need to consider how the product will be used, what materials will be used and the disposal of the product.
- End of life disposal – if a product can be recycled after use, then there is less impact on the environment as less of the raw materials are needed to make new products.
- Plastics can be sorted after they have been used using their recycle number.
- Aluminium can be re-melted into **ingots** and used in other products.
- Glass bottles are usually re-used. They can be sterilised and re-filled, which requires very little processing.
- Glass however does not degrade so can be recycled over and over again.
- If a product does have to go into landfill at the end of its useful life, it should be made from **biodegradable** materials.
- Non-biodegradable materials take hundreds of years to break down.

Obsolete: something which is no longer useful, or out of date.

Ethics: moral principles.

Raw materials: before they have undergone processing, the state a material is first found in (for example, ores from the ground before they are processed into metals).

Ingots: bars of metal that can be processed.

Biodegradable: something which breaks down and degrades naturally.

Exam tip

Make sure that you understand key terminology and can give a definition. This will help you when you attempt multiple choice-style questions.

Typical mistake

If a question asks for a description, comparison or analysis, you will lose marks if your answer lacks depth.

Now test yourself

1 Explain the benefits of using automation in a factory. [4 marks]
2 Explain the term 'virtual retailing'. [2 marks]
3 Give an example of where technology push has produced a new product. [2 marks]
4 Why do designers need to consider the needs of everyone in society when designing a product? [4 marks]
5 Explain the term JIT production. [2 marks]

2 Energy generation and storage

Electricity is our main power supply and we are very dependent upon it. You need to understand how it is supplied and stored, and what alternative fuels are available.

Fossil fuels

REVISED

- Britain relies on **fossil fuels** to provide energy.
- All fuels have to be burnt to produce heat. In electricity generation, heat is used to convert water to steam, which then drives **turbines** connected to **generators**.
- Burning fuel creates CO_2 which adds to the **greenhouse effect**.
- Power stations can be built anywhere to convert fossil fuels into electricity, but they need a water supply.

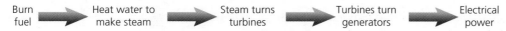

Burn fuel → Heat water to make steam → Steam turns turbines → Turbines turn generators → Electrical power

Figure 2.1 Energy conversion

- Coal – 23 per cent of UK electricity comes from coal-fired power stations, so coal is imported from abroad as deep-pit mining has stopped in Britain.
  - Mining and burning coal releases pollutants into the atmosphere, such as sulphur dioxide.
  - Waste tips, stock piles and open pits look unsightly and are hazardous.
  - The advantage of using coal is that it needs no processing before burning.
- Natural gas – this is Britain's main source of power for electricity production.
  - It is used for heating and cooking and can be used directly without the need for processing. It is transported through pipelines.
  - Methane is the main natural gas and is found deep underground.
  - The majority of Britain's supply comes from pipelines connected to Europe.
- Oil – this is hardly used to produce electricity in Britain.
  - It needs to be processed and refined from crude oil.
  - Stocks of oil will run out before coal.
- Although there are deposits of shale gas under Britain, it is thought that accessing these could pollute our water supplies and cause earthquakes.

> **Fossil fuels**: coal, oil and gas, which are finite resources and are found naturally.
>
> **Greenhouse effect**: pollution in the atmosphere causes the sun's heat to get trapped in the lower atmosphere and warm up the planet.
>
> **Fission**: division or splitting of an atom.
>
> **Turbines**: a wheel inside a machine is rotated by a flow of water, or other fluid, or steam or gas.
>
> **Generators**: machines for converting mechanical energy into electricity.

Nuclear power

REVISED

- **Fission** is the splitting of uranium atoms to produce heat – this occurs in nuclear reactors.
- Huge amounts of energy can be produced in this way from a small quantity of uranium.
- The heat produced is used to heat water and convert it to steam, which is then used to power generators in the same way as with fossil fuels.

- By 2025 the UK's current nuclear power stations are set to have closed as they will have reached the end of their serviceable life.
- It is expensive and potentially dangerous to dispose of power stations, as nuclear material could leak. Nuclear waste is highly hazardous and has long-lasting effects.

Renewable energy `REVISED`

- **Renewable** energy is being looked at more favourably due to the negative environmental impact of using fossil fuels and nuclear energy.
- Renewable energy sources provide 25 per cent of the electricity Britain uses. Very little waste is produced.

Renewable (energy): from a source which will not run out.

Typical mistake

Don't confuse the definitions of renewable and non-renewable – you must be able to give correct examples.

Table 1.2 Renewable energy sources

Renewable energy source	How power is generated
Wind	<ul><li>Windmills – tall towers with propeller-like blades – drive a generator.</li><li>Several windmills are grouped together to create a wind farm.</li><li>Coastlines, hilltops and between hills and mountains are the best places for harvesting wind.</li></ul>
Solar	<ul><li>Photovoltaic panels collect solar energy.</li><li>They take up valuable space and are therefore often placed on roofs and sides of tall buildings.</li><li>They are most effective nearer the equator.</li></ul>
Tidal	<ul><li>The gravitational pull of the moon causes changes in water levels (tides).</li><li>A tidal barrier (or 'estuary bridge') is a long dam built across the mouth of a river where it meets the sea – turbines within it collect energy from the tide as it passes through, generating electricity.</li><li>A disadvantage is that rivers never empty and mudflats can flood, ruining birds' habitats</li></ul>
Hydroelectricity	<ul><li>A dam is used to block a river and create a water reserve. This is stored in a reservoir and channelled through turbines, which turn generators.</li><li>Electricity can be produced very quickly.</li></ul>
Wave	<ul><li>Energy provided by the up and down movement of a wave is either converted into mechanical energy to move pistons or compress air to force it through a turbine.</li><li>This energy is difficult to collect.</li></ul>
Biomass	<ul><li>Plants are grown to burn, or decaying plants and animal matter are used to produce heat.</li><li>Oilseed rape and willow are harvested as biomass crops and can be regrown quickly.</li><li>Some vegetable oils are treated after cooking to use for diesel engines.</li><li>Burning plants causes atmospheric pollution (but is less harmful than burning fossil fuels).</li></ul>

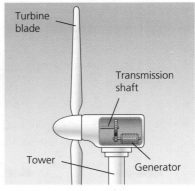

Figure 2.2 Wind turbines are now commonly used in Britain

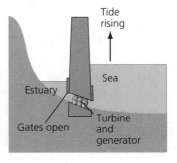
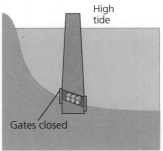
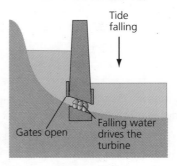

Figure 2.3 Tidal energy

Exam practice answers at **www.hoddereducation.co.uk/6 myrevisionnotesdownloads**

Energy storage systems

- Energy can be stored to be used at a later date.
- Kinetic pumped storage – this storage method can deal with a sudden high demand for electricity. It can be used as an additional fast-acting electricity top-up system, as both nuclear and coal power stations are slow to respond.

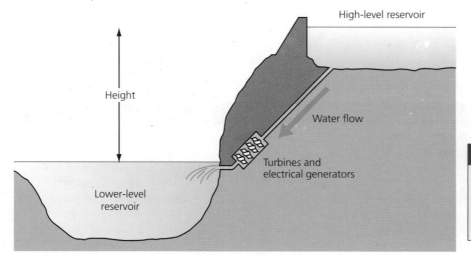

Figure 2.4 Kinetic energy conversion

○ Figure 2.4 shows a hydroelectric dam system set across two levels. The pumped storage system releases water from the higher reservoir to the lower one through turbines which turn generators and produce electricity.

○ As coal and nuclear power stations cannot reduce their output at low times (night-time), this energy is used at a cheaper cost to pump the water back up to the top reservoir.

- Batteries – there are two main types: primary or single use (which get thrown away) and secondary or rechargeable.

○ Batteries provide electrical energy away from a mains supply, so are useful in portable products.

○ Primary batteries are alkaline and zinc-carbon and typically produce about 1.5 volts per cell.

○ Rechargeable batteries are more expensive to buy than single-use batteries, but are cost-efficient in the long run as they don't need to be replaced, only recharged.

> **Typical mistake**
>
> Don't use generic terms such as 'battery' without giving specific details or terminology and uses.

> **Exam tip**
>
> Understand the advantages and disadvantages of each type of energy and storage to score higher marks, so that you are able to draw comparisons and make conclusions.

Now test yourself

1 Explain a way of producing electricity in a series of stages. [5 marks]
2 Discuss the problems associated with the use of biomass as a renewable energy source. [2 marks]
3 List three ways to store energy, and describe one in detail. [3 marks]

3 Developments in new materials

Modern materials

Modern materials are materials that have been produced through the invention or discovery of new processes. A designer will make use of these to make new and improved products.

Table 3.1 Modern materials, their properties and applications

Modern material	Description	Properties	Applications
Graphene	Graphene is a two-dimensional layer of carbon. It is harder than diamond, 300 times stronger than steel and is currently the lightest known material.	Very lightweight Transparent Flexible Tough Very good conductor of electricity	The use of graphene is in development but potential applications include solar-powered smartphones that charge in seconds and water filters that will produce clean water for everyone.
Metal foam	Metal foam is produced by injecting gas into metal when it is in a molten state.	Very lightweight High compressive strength Porous Excellent energy-absorbing properties	Soundproofing in cars As a crash protection safety feature
Titanium	Titanium is a relatively new metal.	High strength to density ratio Excellent resistance to corrosion	Surgical instruments and replacement body parts such as hip joints
Liquid crystal display (LCD)	An LCD is a laminate of two layers of glass with a liquid crystal core.	Opaque (when an electrical current is applied to the liquid crystal core)	Flat screen televisions
Nano materials	Nano materials are very, very small: one-billionth of a metre in size. They are added to other materials to improve their properties.	Can be coated onto glass to make it 'self-cleaning' Can be added to sports equipment to make it lighter and stronger Antibacterial qualities	Glass, sports equipment, antibacterial socks
Polytetrafluorethylene (PTFE)	PTFE is a non-stick coating applied to surfaces to make then slippery.	Non-stick	Kitchen utensils and pans (these are often coated 'Teflon')
Corn starch polymers	Corn starch polymers are made from polylactic acid that is found in potatoes, corn and maze. It is an alternative to oil-based polymers.	Renewable Biodegradable	Disposable cutlery and food packaging

Modern material	Description	Properties	Applications
Anodised aluminium	A coating applied to aluminium by an electrolytic process.	Hardens the surface of aluminium. It can have a dye applied to change the appearance of the aluminium.	Sports drinks bottles, components for climbing equipment and mountain bikes
Nickel plating	A coating applied to metal by an electrolytic process.	Prevents corrosion and wear of the base metal	Door handles, belt buckles, nuts and bolts
Polymer-coated steel	A coating of a thermoforming polymer applied to hot metal.	Prevents corrosion and alters the appearance of the base metal	Tool handles

Figure 3.1 Anodised carabiners

Smart materials

A **smart material** can have its properties altered by a change in external stimuli. This can be by heat, light, stress, moisture or pH.

- **Shape memory alloys (SMAs)** will return to their original shape when heated.
- **Thermochromatic** pigments change colour at varying temperatures.

Figure 3.2 These babies' feeding spoons change colour when heated

- **Photochromic** pigments change colour depending on how much light is present.

Modern material: a material that has recently been developed.

Smart material: a material that reacts to environmental changes such as heat and light.

Shape memory alloy (SMA): a metal that will return to its original shape when placed in hot water.

Thermochromatic: a material that reacts to heat.

Photochromic: a material that reacts to light.

Typical mistake

It is easy to confuse the terms 'modern material' and 'smart material' under the pressure of the exam. Make sure you know the difference to prevent losing marks.

Composite materials

A **composite material** is made up of two or more materials, and is designed to enhance the properties of the material.

● Glass-reinforced polymer (GRP) is made from strands of glass mixed with a polyester resin. This produces a strong, mouldable material that is tough and waterproof. It is commonly used to manufacture canoes, boat hulls and 'kit cars'.

● Carbon-fibre reinforced plastic (CFRP) is very similar to GRP but uses carbon fibre instead of stands of glass. This makes it lightweight and very strong. It is used in the production of Formula One racing cars and expensive bicycles.

Technical textiles

Technical textiles are manufactured for their functional capabilities rather than their aesthetic appearance.

● **Conductive fabrics** have conductive fibres or conductive powders impregnated into them. They allow electrical currents to be passed through them. Fencing suits use '**e-textiles**' to record a score.

● Fire-resistant fabrics use meta-aramid to increase their resistance to fire. A firefighter's suit uses this material to help protect the user from flames while still being flexible and breathable.

● Kevlar is a combination of terephthaloyl chloride and para-phenylenediamine mixed with a layer of resin. This produces a very light, very strong material that can withstand extremes of temperature. This makes it an ideal material for the manufacture of bulletproof vests and safety clothing.

● Microfibres are very fine synthetic fibres that are used for outdoor clothing and sportswear. They are breathable, durable, crease-resistant and easy to care for.

> **Exam tip**
>
> Make sure that you know the name of at least one modern material, one smart material, one composite material and one technical textile. Be ready to give uses for that material and explain its properties.

> **Composite material**: a material that combines the properties of two or more materials.
>
> **Technical textiles**: textiles manufactured for their functional capabilities.
>
> **Conductive fabrics**: textiles that conduct electricity.
>
> **E-textiles**: textiles that use smart materials.

Now test yourself

1 Give the name of a suitable protective coating for aluminium. [1 mark]
2 Explain the advantages of using corn starch polymers for food packaging. [4 marks]
3 What is meant by the term 'smart material'? [2 marks]
4 Explain why carbon fibre reinforced plastic is used to manufacture the body of a Formula One racing car. [4 marks]
5 Give the name of a technical textile and suggest a suitable use. [2 marks]

4 Systems approach to designing

- Electronic systems are used to provide functionality to products and processes.
- A **system** is a set of parts that work together.
- Electronic systems have three different elements: input, process and output.
- A systems diagram is used to show how an operation breaks down into these three elements and to describe what is happening in a system.

Figure 4.1 This systems diagram shows the input, process and output for a street light sensor

Inputs

- **Input devices** are electrical and/or mechanical sensors.
- They use signals from the environment (for example, heat, light or pressure) and convert them into signals that can be passed to processing devices and components.
- A **light-dependent resistor (LDR)** is an input device used to detect light levels.
- When levels of light are low, resistance is high and low levels of electrical current flow through it; in intense light, it has low resistance and the level of current flowing increases.
- LDRs are used in street lights, night lights and clock radios.
- A temperature sensor or **thermistor** is a component in which resistance changes with changes in temperature.
- In some thermistors, resistance increases when temperature increases; in others, resistance falls when temperature increases.
- Thermistors are used in toasters, refrigerators and hairdryers.
- Pressure sensors – resistance changes with changes in pressure.
- **Switches** are useful input devices that sense when pressure is applied. Different types are used in many different products.

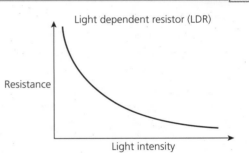

Figure 4.2 An LDR's resistance decreases as light intensity increases

> **System**: a set of parts or components that work together and provide functionality to products and processes.
>
> **Input device**: an electrical or mechanical sensor that uses signals from the environment and converts them into signals that can be passed to processing devices and components.
>
> **Light-dependent resistor (LDR)**: an input device used to detect light levels in which resistance increases in low light and decreases in intense light.
>
> **Thermistor**: an input device in which resistance changes with changes in temperature.
>
> **Switch**: an input device that senses when pressure is applied.

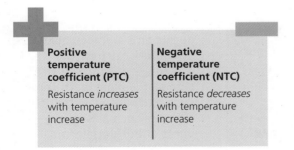

Positive temperature coefficient (PTC)	Negative temperature coefficient (NTC)
Resistance *increases* with temperature increase	Resistance *decreases* with temperature increase

Figure 4.3 Thermistors either increase or decrease resistance when they detect increases in temperature

Processes

- **Process devices** handle information received from an input device and turn outputs on and/or off.
- In electronic systems, processes are often controlled by an **integrated circuit (IC)**.
- A **microcontroller** is the most frequently used IC; it is a small computer within a single IC used to provide functionality to a product.
- Microcontrollers can be used as counters, timers and for decision-making in electronic systems.
- Designers often use flowcharts with standard symbols to describe the operation of a program.

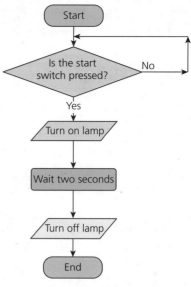

Figure 4.4 This flowchart describes a program that flashes an LED on and off

Outputs

- **Output devices** send out information (such as, heat, light, sound or movement) to the environment.
- Lamps pass electric current through a thin tungsten filament that operates in a glass bulb. They produce a lot of light and heat but have poor energy efficiency and have been replaced by LEDs in many products.
- Buzzers and speakers are sound output devices often used in alarm devices and timers. They can also confirm user input such as a button press or a mouse click.
- **Light-emitting diodes (LEDs)** are usually round and 5 mm in diameter (although they are available in a range of shapes, sizes and colours). They are very bright and often used as indicators on control panels.

Process device: a device that handles information received from an input device and turn outputs on and/or off.

Integrated circuit (IC): a self-contained circuit made up of separate components that act as process devices in an electronic system.

Microcontroller: a small computer with a single integrated circuit used to provide functionality and control.

Output device: a device that sends out information to the environment.

Light-emitting diode (LED): an output device that produces light.

> **Typical mistake**
>
> Try not to confuse the functions of microcontrollers and microprocessors. *Microcontrollers* are used in integrated circuits to run a set sequence of instructions. *Microprocessors* used in computers carry out many different tasks.

Now test yourself

1 Name three input devices. [3 marks]
2 Explain how an LDR works. [2 marks]
3 State what the input device would be in a system designed to alert a person to an intruder in their home. [1 mark]
4 Describe how a microcontroller is used in an electronic system. [2 marks]
5 Name three output devices. [3 marks]

> **Exam tip**
>
> Questions on electronic systems may describe a system and ask you to decide on a suitable input or output device for the system. To prepare for this type of question, learn some system diagrams for simple systems such as security lights or burglar alarms.

5 Mechanical devices

A **mechanism** is a device that changes an input motion into an output motion.

Different types of movement

There are four different types of movement:

- **Linear** motion – movement in a straight line: for example, a conveyor belt
- **Rotary** motion – movement round in a circle: for example, a wheel
- **Reciprocating** motion – movement backwards and forwards in a straight line: for example, a needle in a sewing machine
- **Oscillating** motion – movement swinging from side to side: for example, a pendulum in a clock.

Changing magnitude and direction of force

Mechanisms can change the amount of movement and the direction of movement.

Levers

- A **lever** is a simple mechanism that changes an *input* motion and force into an *output* motion and force.
- The input force is called the **effort**. This is the force applied to move the object.
- The output is called the **load**. This is the object to be moved.
- A lever moves around a fixed point called a **pivot** or **fulcrum**.

There are three types or orders of lever:

- A **first-order lever** has the fulcrum anywhere between the effort and the load. The closer the fulcrum is to the load, the less effort needed to move it.

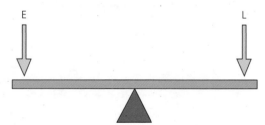

Figure 5.1 A seesaw is an example of a first-order lever

- A **second-order lever** has the load and effort on the same side of the fulcrum. Because the load is nearer the fulcrum, less effort is needed to move it. An example would be a wheelbarrow.

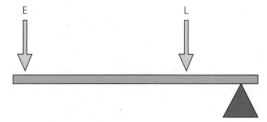

Figure 5.2 A second-order lever

> **Mechanism**: a device that changes an input motion into an output motion.
>
> **Linear motion**: movement in a straight line.
>
> **Rotary motion**: movement round in a circle.
>
> **Reciprocating motion**: movement backwards and forwards in a straight line.
>
> **Oscillating motion**: movement swinging from side to side.
>
> **Lever**: a simple mechanism that changes an input motion and force into an output motion and force.
>
> **Effort**: an input force applied to move an object.
>
> **Load**: an output force.
>
> **Pivot** or **fulcrum**: a fixed point around which a mechanism moves.
>
> **First-order lever**: a lever that has the fulcrum anywhere between the effort and the load.
>
> **Second-order lever**: a lever that has the load and effort on the same side of the fulcrum.

- A **third-order lever** has the load and effort on the same side of the fulcrum, but the load is further away from the fulcrum and therefore the effort needed is greater than the load. Barbeque tongs would be an example of a third-order lever.

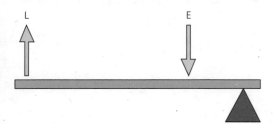

Figure 5.3 A third-order lever

Rotary systems

- Mechanisms that control and change rotary motion have a turning force that causes rotation, which is called **torque**.
- Rotary mechanisms can either reduce rotary speed and increase torque, or increase rotary speed and reduce torque.

Cams and followers

- A **cam and follower** converts rotary motion into reciprocating motion: when the cam rotates, the follower moves up and down.
- The pattern in which the follower moves up and down is controlled by the shape of the cam.
- The follower can rise (go up), fall (go down) or dwell (stay still).

Simple gear trains

- A **gear train** is a mechanism that transmits rotary motion and torque.
- A gear train has a driver gear (input) and a driven gear (output) – these are wheels that have teeth around the edge that interlock.
- Different sized gears connected together either increase or decrease the speed of rotation and increase or decrease the torque.
- The smaller gear will rotate faster than the larger gear.
- The gears will rotate in opposite directions.

Linkages

- A **linkage** is a mechanism that transfers force and changes the direction of movement.
- The number and shapes of the linkages can change the direction of the force.
- The position of the pivots can change the size or magnitude of the force.
- A **bell crank linkage** changes the direction of the input motion through 90°.
- It has one fixed pivot and two moving pivots.
- In a **push/pull** linkage (or **parallel motion** linkage), the direction of motion and the magnitude of the forces are the same.
- It has two fixed pivots and four moving pivots.

> **Third-order lever**: a lever that has the load and effort on the same side of the fulcrum, but the load is further away from the fulcrum and therefore the effort needed is greater than the load.
>
> **Torque**: a turning force that causes rotation.

Typical mistake

Don't be confused about the direction of movement in different rotary systems. Remember that in gear trains the gears move in the *opposite* direction, but belts and pulleys move in the *same* direction.

> **Cam and follower**: a mechanism that converts rotary motion into reciprocating motion when the cam rotates and the follower moves up and down.
>
> **Gear train**: a mechanism with two wheels with teeth around the edge that interlock and transmit rotary motion and torque.

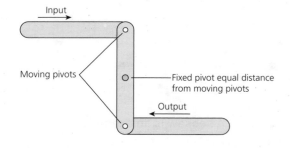

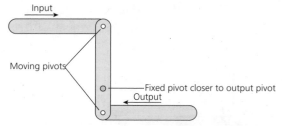

Figure 5.4 The shape of the linkage can change the direction of force, and the position of the pivots can change the magnitude of the force

 Exam practice answers at **www.hoddereducation.co.uk/6 myrevisionnotesdownloads**

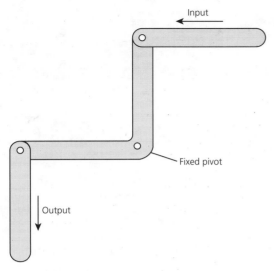

Figure 5.5 **A bell crank linkage changes the direction of the input motion through 90°**

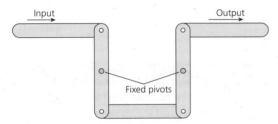

Figure 5.6 **In a push/pull linkage the input and output motion are in the same direction**

Pulleys and belts

- **Pulleys** (wheels with grooves in their rim) **and belts** (which connect two pulleys) transmit rotary motion to rotary motion.
- Different sized pulleys connected together either increase or decrease the speed of rotation and increase or decrease the torque transmitted.
- When the driver pulley is larger than the driven pulley, the driven pulley will spin faster but the torque will be less.
- When the driver pulley is smaller than the driven pulley, the driven pulley will spin slower but the torque will be increased.

5 Mechanical devices

Linkage: a mechanism that transfers force and changes the direction of movement.

Bell crank linkage: a linkage that changes the direction of the input motion through 90°.

Push/pull or **parallel motion linkage**: a linkage in which the direction of motion and the magnitude of the forces are the same.

Pulleys and belts: a mechanism of two small wheels connected by a belt that transmit rotary motion to rotary motion.

Exam tip

Questions are likely to test your knowledge of the functions of mechanical devices to produce different sorts of movement and to change the magnitude and direction of forces. Make sure you know the types of movement each different mechanical device produces, and – for linkages and rotary systems – how they change the size and direction of force.

Now test yourself

TESTED ☐

1. Give an example of an object that moves in an oscillating motion. [1 mark]
2. Give an example of a second-order lever. [1 mark]
3. Explain what is meant by torque. [2 marks]
4. Explain how a cam and follower mechanism works and the types of motion it transmits. [3 marks]
5. Describe the speed of motion and size of torque in a pulley and belt system that has a small driver pulley and a larger driven pulley. [2 marks]

6 Materials and their working properties

Papers and boards

- Papers and boards are used to manufacture a wide range of products.
- They are made from **cellulose** fibres found in plants, which is a **renewable** source.
- Papers and boards are usually made from part-**recycled** materials.
- The properties of paper and board can be changed to make it a more useful material (waterproofing, for example).
- Paper is measured from A0 to A6 and in grams per square metre (gsm). Anything weighing less than 200 gsm is classified as paper.
- Boards are always heavier than 200 gsm.
- Corrugated card is a lightweight yet strong material as it contains a fluted structure in the middle layer. It is used for packaging for this reason.

> **Cellulose**: fibres found in plant materials.
>
> **Renewable**: a source of material that if managed responsibly will not run out.
>
> **Recycled**: material which has had another use or purpose previously and has been reprocessed and made into a new product.

Table 6.1 **Papers and their uses**

Paper	Properties	Common uses
Bleed proof	Smooth paper, often used with water and spirit-based markers Prevents marker bleed (when ink runs and seeps through the paper)	Used for presentation drawings
Cartridge paper	Good quality white paper often with a slight texture Available in different weights	Due to the good-quality surface, it can be used for paints and markers as well as drawing
Grid	Paper printed with different grids as guidelines (These can be isometric or differently-sized grids.)	Quick model making and working drawings
Layout paper	Thin translucent lightweight paper Can be drawn on with markers and takes colours well	Initial quick sketching and tracing
Tracing paper	Thin, transparent paper	Tracing copies of drawings

Table 6.2 **Boards and their uses**

Board	Properties	Common uses
Corrugated card	Strong, lightweight material Made up of two or more layers and a fluted middle section leading to good insulating properties Available in different thicknesses	Packaging such as pizza boxes and large boxes used for heavy items that need protecting
Duplex board	Thin board which often has one side that is suitable for printing	Food packaging
Foil-lined board	Board covered on one side with aluminium foil, making it a good insulator of heat	Takeaway or ready-meal packaging
Foam-core board	Two pieces of board with a core of foam to increase the thickness Thick board that is very lightweight	Model making, such as architectural models
Inkjet card	Treated so it can be used in all inkjet printers	Printing in inkjet printers
Solid white board	Top quality cardboard, smooth and white Good for printing on	Book covers

Natural and manufactured timbers

Timber is a natural product that has the benefit of being renewable. By understanding the properties of different types of timber you will be able to make an informed choice on which one to use when designing and making products.

- Natural timber is categorised into two groups: **hardwoods** and **softwoods**.
- Hardwoods come from deciduous trees that have broad leaves that generally fall in autumn.
- Hardwoods are generally harder, more expensive, more durable and take longer to grow than softwoods.

Table 6.3 Types of hardwood

Hardwood	Properties	Common uses
Ash	Tough and flexible Wide grained Finishes well	Sports equipment, ladders
Beech	Hard and strong Close grain Prone to warping and splitting	Furniture, children's toys, workshop tool handles and bench tops
Mahogany	Strong and durable Available in wide planks Fairly easy to work but can have interlocking grain	Good quality furniture, panelling and veneers
Oak	Hard, tough and durable Open grain Can be finished to a high standard	Timber framed buildings, high quality furniture, flooring
Balsa	Strong and durable Lightweight, easy to work	Model making, floats and rafts

- Softwoods come from coniferous trees that have needle type leaves and keep their leaves all year.
- Softwoods are generally easier to work and, as they grow faster than hardwoods, are considered to be more sustainable than hardwoods.

Table 6.4 Types of softwood

Softwood	Properties	Common uses
Larch	Reddish in colour and has a striking grain pattern Tough but easy to work, although quite resinous and prone to splitting Naturally resistant to rot	Fencing, fence posts, cladding and decking
Pine	Straight grained, light yellow in colour Soft and easy to work Can be quite knotty	Interior joinery and furniture, window frames
Spruce	Creamy white in colour Easy to work with small knots Lightweight with good resonant properties	Bedroom furniture, stringed musical instruments

Manufactured boards – timber which is manufactured into large boards by either laminating or by compression.

Advantages over natural timber:

- available in large sheets: 2,440 mm by 1,220 mm (8 ft x 4 ft)
- stable, less likely to warp, twist, shrink or bow
- smooth, flat surface
- suited to CNC machining.

> **Hardwoods**: come from deciduous trees and are generally hard and durable.
>
> **Softwoods**: come from coniferous trees that are relatively fast growing.
>
> **Manufactured boards**: man-made boards that come in large sizes and are usually flat and stable.

Table 6.5 **Types of manufactured boards**

Manufactured board	Description	Properties
Medium density fibreboard (MDF)	Made from compressed fine wood fibres bonded together with resin	This board is relatively inexpensive and has a flat, smooth surface
Plywood	Made from wood veneers glued together with alternating grain	Very strong, with a flat, smooth surface
Chipboard	Made from wood chips bonded together with resin	Inexpensive construction material

Metals and alloys

REVISED

Metal is a naturally-occurring material that is found in the ground in the form of ore. It is non-renewable but generally easy to recycle. Different metals have very different properties and are categorised into **ferrous** and **non-ferrous** metals.

Table 6.6 **Ferrous metals**

Ferrous metal	Composition	Properties	Common uses
Low carbon steel (mild steel)	Iron and 0.15–0.35% carbon	Good tensile strength, tough, malleable Poor resistance to corrosion	Car bodies, nuts, bolts, and screws, RSJs and girders
Cast iron	Iron and 3.5% carbon	Hard surface but has a brittle soft core Strong compressive strength Cheap	Vices, car brake discs, cylinder blocks, manhole covers
High carbon steel (tool steel)	Iron and 0.70–1.4% carbon	Hard but also brittle Less tough, malleable or ductile than medium carbon steel	Screwdrivers, chisels, taps and dies

Table 6.7 **Non-ferrous metals**

Non-ferrous metal	Properties	Common uses
Aluminium	Lightweight, soft, ductile and malleable A good conductor of heat and electricity Corrosion-resistant	Aircraft bodies, high-end car chassis, cans, cooking pans, bike frames
Copper	Extremely ductile and malleable An excellent conductor of heat and electricity Easily soldered and corrosion-resistant	Plumbing fittings, hot water tanks, electrical wire
Tin	Soft, ductile and malleable Low melting point Excellent corrosion resistance	Coatings on food and drinks cans, solders

Non-ferrous metal	Properties	Common uses
Zinc	Weak in its pure state High level of corrosion resistance Low melting point Easily worked	As a galvanised coating in crash barriers, corrugated roofing, intricate die-cast products

- **Alloys** can be ferrous or non-ferrous.

Table 6.8 **Alloys**

Alloy	Composition	Properties	Common uses
Brass – non-ferrous alloy	Alloy of copper (65%) and zinc (35%)	Strong and ductile Casts well Corrosion-resistant Conductor of heat and electricity	Castings, forgings, taps, wood screws
Stainless steel – ferrous alloy	Alloy of steel also including chromium (18%), nickel (8%) and magnesium (8%)	Hard and tough Excellent resistance to corrosion	Sinks, cutlery, surgical equipment, homewares
Duralumin	Alloy of aluminum (90%), copper (4%), magnesium (1%), manganese (0.5–1%)	Strong, soft and malleable Excellent corrosion resistance Lightweight	Aircraft structure and fixings, suspension applications, fuel tanks

Ferrous metals: metals that contain iron, are magnetic but are prone to rusting.

Non-ferrous metals: metals that do not contain iron and therefore do not rust.

Alloy: a mixture of two or more metals designed to improve the quality of the metal for a given purpose.

Polymers

REVISED

The majority of polymers that we use are refined from crude oil. This means that they are non-renewable but many are recyclable. Polymers are categorised into **thermoforming polymers** and **thermosetting polymers**.

- Thermoforming polymers have the advantage of being able to be repeatedly formed and reformed with the use of heat.
- They can have additives to improve their working properties, and pigments added to alter their appearance.

Table 6.9 **Thermoforming polymers**

Thermoforming polymer	Properties	Common uses
Acrylic (PMMA)	Hard Excellent optical quality Good resistance to weathering Scratches easily	Car-light units, bath tubs, shop signage and displays
High impact polystyrene (HIPS)	Tough, hard and rigid Good impact resistance Lightweight	Children's toys, yoghurt pots, refrigerator liners

Thermoforming polymer	Properties	Common uses
High-density polythene (HDPE)	Hard and stiff Excellent chemical resistance	Washing-up bowls, buckets, milk crates, bottles and pipes
Polypropylene (PP)	Tough Good heat and chemical resistance Lightweight Fatigue-resistant	Toys, DVD and Blu-ray cases, food packaging film, bottle caps and medical equipment
Polyvinyl chloride (PVC)	Hard and tough Good chemical and weather resistance Low cost Can be rigid or flexible	Pipes, guttering, window frames
Polyethylene terephthalate (PET)	Tough and durable Lightweight Food safe Impermeable to water Low cost	Drinks bottles, food packaging

- Thermosetting polymers can also be shaped and formed with heat, but once set they cannot be reshaped. Unfortunately, this makes them very difficult to recycle.

Table 6.10 Thermosetting polymers

Thermosetting polymer	Properties	Common uses
Epoxy resin	Electrical insulator Good chemical and wear resistance	Adhesives such as Araldite™, PCB component encapsulation
Melamine formaldehyde (MF)	Stiff, hard and strong Excellent resistance to heat, scratching and staining	Kitchen work-surface laminates, tableware
Phenol formaldehyde (PF)	Hard Heat- and chemical-resistant Good electrical insulator Limited colours available	Electrical fittings, saucepan handles, bowling balls
Polyester resin	Brittle but becomes tough when laminated with glass fibre Hard and resistant to UV	GRP boats, car body panels
Urea formaldehyde (UF)	Stiff and hard Heat-resistant Good electrical insulator	White electrical fittings, toilet seats, adhesive used in MDF

Thermoforming polymers: polymers that can be formed and shaped with the use of heat.

Thermosetting polymers: polymers that once formed cannot be reformed with the use of heat.

Textiles

Fabrics and textiles are used for much more than clothing and there are many different types of fibre and fabric available.

The starting point for all fabrics is the fibre, which is a very fine, hair-like structure, and the fibre's properties will vary depending on where it comes from.

Designers need to be aware of the different fabrics when selecting one for a specific product.

- **Natural fibres** come from plants (for example, cotton) and animals (for example, wool and silk).

Table 6.11 Natural fibres

Cotton	Good strength, very absorbent, creases and shrinks, poor insulator, very flammable
Wool	Moderate strength, very absorbent, good crease-resistance, can shrink badly, good insulator, not very flammable
Silk	Good strength, very absorbent, can crease badly but natural elasticity helps it shed creases, warm and cool to wear, not very flammable

- **Synthetic fibres** are made from oil-based chemicals (for example, polyester, nylon and elastane).

Table 6.12 Synthetic fibres

Polyamide	Very strong and abrasion-resistant, non-absorbent, does not crease or shrink, slight elasticity, poor insulator, melts but does not burn, **thermoplastic**
Polyester	Very strong and abrasion-resistant, non-absorbent, does not crease or shrink, no elasticity, poor insulator, melts but does not burn, thermoplastic
Elastane	Good strength, non-absorbent, does not crease or shrink, very high elasticity, poor insulator, does not burn

- **Blended fabrics** are often used to get the best out of each fibre. Polyester is often blended with cotton and other fibres as it reduces absorbency, creasing and shrinking, and adds strength and thermoplastic qualities to the fabric.
- Woven textiles: the plain weave is the simplest structure and makes strong fabrics with a smooth surface that is good for printing on.
- **Non-woven fabrics** are made directly from layers of fibres and include felt and bonded fabrics.
- Bonded fabrics are made from webs of fibres held together in various ways.
- Felts are made using the natural felting ability of wool fibres.
- Knitted fabrics are made of interlocked loops of yarn.

Natural fibres: fibres from plant and animal sources.

Synthetic fibres: fibres manufactured from oil-based chemicals.

Thermoplastic fibres: these soften when heated and can be heat-set into new shapes.

Blended fabrics: containing two or more different fibres.

Non-woven fabrics: these are made directly from fibres without the need to make them into yarns first.

Exam tip

When asked to give an example of a fibre or fabric for a specific use, think about the qualities needed in the product, such as strength or absorbency, to help you choose one that is right. It might help to remember that natural fibres have almost the opposite qualities to synthetic fibres. For example, natural fibres are good at absorbing moisture but synthetic fibres are almost totally non-absorbent.

Typical mistake

Many students confuse woven and knitted structures; the yarns in woven fabrics are interlaced but are looped together in knitted fabrics.

Table 6.13 Fabric Structures

Woven fabrics	Little stretch, usually have good strength, poor insulators, can crease easily, can fray
Non-woven fabrics	Poor stretch, poor strength, poor insulators, poor crease-resistance, do not fray
Knitted fabrics	Good stretch, moderate strength, good insulators in still air but poor in moving air, have good resistance to creasing, do not fray but weft knit structure can ladder

Material properties

REVISED

Material properties need to be considered to select the correct material for the job.

A material's physical properties describe how that material will behave under specific conditions.

- Absorbency – how well a material soaks up and retains liquids, heat or light. This is an important property of most fabrics.
- Density – a material's mass per unit volume.
- Fusibility – how easily a material's state can be turned into a liquid (solder melts with the heat of a soldering iron due to a low melting point).
- Electrical conductivity – how easily electrical energy can be passed through a material (for example, gold is an excellent conductor).
- Thermal conductivity – how easily a material allows heat to pass through it. (Aluminium has good thermal conductivity and is used in pans.)

A material's mechanical properties describe how it will behave when being worked or shaped.

- Strength – a material's ability to withstand a constant force without breaking. Strength is linked to the five forces that can act upon a material (tension, compression, torsion, shear and bending).

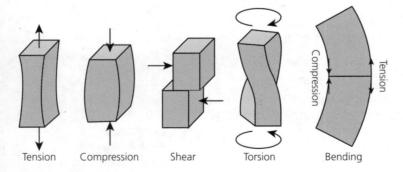

Figure 6.1 Forces

Exam practice answers at www.hoddereducation.co.uk/6 myrevisionnotesdownloads

- Hardness – the ability to withstand scratching, cutting and abrasion. (Melamine is used for kitchen work surfaces due to its hardness.)
- Toughness – a material's ability to withstand impact. (HDPE is used to make toys due to its toughness).
- Malleability – a material's ability to be permanently deformed or shaped by impact, rolling or pressing, without breaking. (Low carbon steel is used on car body panels as they can be pressed into shape.)
- Ductility – the ability to be pulled or drawn into a fine wire without breaking. (Copper used to make wire is ductile).
- Elasticity – a material's ability to be stretched under force and to return to its original shape. (Lycra is used in sportswear as it can stretch to fit the body.)

Typical mistake

Don't mix up the categories of the different types of materials – such as stating that oak is a softwood, brass is a pure ferrous metal, or acrylic (PMMA) is a thermosetting polymer.

Exam tip

Make sure that you can visually identify materials from a photograph and that you know the properties and uses of a range of different woods, metals, polymers and textiles.

Now test yourself

TESTED ☐

1 Give the name of a paper/board used for packaging and the properties which make it suitable. [2 marks]
2 For a mechanical and a physical property of your choice, give a definition of each and an example of a material that has that property. [4 marks]
3 List three features of a coniferous tree. [3 marks]
4 Name a suitable polymer for a water bottle. [1 mark]
5 Explain why most aircraft are made using aluminium. [3 marks]
6 What is the source of synthetic fibres? [1 mark]
7 Give three reasons why fibres are often blended before being made into a fabric. [3 marks]

Exam practice

1 Which of these statements is true?
  a) Cotton fibres are very flammable.
  b) Polyester is an absorbent fibre.
  c) Polyester fibres are very elastic.
  d) Wool fibres come from a plant. [1 mark]

2 Give the correct definition for the term 'hardness'.
  a) The ability to withstand bending
  b) The ability to withstand impact
  c) The ability to withstand scratching
  d) The ability to withstand twisting [1 mark]

3 Which of the following explains why corrugated card is used in packaging?
  a) It is aesthetically pleasing.
  b) It is inexpensive.
  c) It is lightweight.
  d) It is waterproof. [1 mark]

4 Which of the following fibres is thermoplastic?
  a) Cotton   c) Silk
  b) Polyamide   d) Wool [1 mark]

5 Which of the following is not a type of weave?
  a) Plain   c) Twill
  b) Satin   d) Weft [1 mark]

6 Describe a way to enhance the properties of paper/card. [1 mark]

7 State two reasons why polyamide fabrics are used for car seatbelts. [2 marks]

8 Name two staple fibres. [2 marks]

9 State two reasons why wool fabrics can be unpopular with consumers. [2 marks]

10 State two reasons why elastane fibres are used in swimwear fabrics. [2 marks]

11 State two reasons why fabrics made from a blend of cotton and polyester fibres are dangerous when set alight. [2 marks]

12 Name the four types of mechanical motion. [4 marks]

13 Describe what is meant by the term 'finite resource'. [1 mark]

14 Give two advantages of using corn starch polymers. [2 marks]

15 What is a composite material? [2 marks]

16 Name two electronic/mechanical input devices. [2 marks]

17 Draw a parallel motion linkage. [2 marks]

18 Give the properties of balsa and suggest a possible use. [3 marks]

19 Give a definition of the term 'ferrous metal'. [1 mark]

20 Give the properties of stainless steel and suggest a possible use. [3 marks]

21 Which one of the following is a thermoforming polymer?
  a) Acrylic (PMMA)   c) Polyester resin
  b) Epoxy resin   d) Phenol formaldehyde [1 mark]

ONLINE

7 Timber-based materials

In the exam you will only need to answer questions on this content in relation to one material category or system. You only need to revise this topic if you plan to answer questions with a focus on timber-based materials.

Selection of materials and components

REVISED

There are many different types of timber and manufactured boards, and each has its own specific properties. It is important to choose the right one for its intended purpose.

Functionality

- A garden bench needs to be strong, durable and weatherproof.
- A child's toy needs to be tough and free from splinters.
- Low-cost furniture needs to be flat, stable and easy to assemble at home.

Aesthetics

- A boardroom table should have a rich, deep colour to give the impression of importance and wealth.
- There is an infinite range of wood colours from sycamore (very pale) to ebony (black).
- Timber can be stained, painted and have a gloss, satin or matt finish.
- Timber is very tactile; it has a natural grain that can be sanded smooth or left quite rough.
- Timber is 'warm' to the touch.

Environmental factors

- Timber is very environmentally friendly as it can be renewed by growing more trees.
- It is biodegradable and will not harm the environment when it is disposed of.
- It is relatively easily to repair and most timbers have a good lifespan.

Availability

- Softwoods are relatively quick growing and there is an abundance of renewable timber.
- Hardwoods take longer to grow.
- Most timber comes in stock sizes which makes designing and making easier to plan.
- Manufactured boards come in large stock sizes and a variety of thicknesses.

Cost

- Timber is a cost-effective material with softwoods and manufactured boards being relatively cheap to purchase.
- Labour-intensive manufacturing costs can increase the price of wooden products.
- Some exotic hardwoods, such as burr walnut, can very expensive.
- Bulk buying of timber can reduce the cost of the material.

Social factors

- Timber is a very accessible, affordable material.
- It is used in all countries as a building and construction material, providing inclusive housing and furniture for everyone.

Cultural factors

- Different cultures have different needs and tastes regarding timber-based products.
- The Japanese make extensive use of bamboo as a timber-based construction material.
- In Northern Europe, log cabins are made from spruce.

Ethical factors

- Timber creates few ethical issues as it is a natural, renewable material.
- However, If timber forests are not managed, this can lead to deforestation.
- Deforestation can cause the loss of habitats for wildlife and can be a contributor to global warming.

Forces and stresses REVISED

Timber is a good construction material and can withstand an impressive amount of force and stress. Different construction techniques can be used to enhance the strength of timber-based materials.

Materials and objects can be manipulated to resist and work with forces and stresses

- Beech has excellent strength and is used for wooden mallets and workbenches.
- Oak has excellent compressive and bending strength and is used in timber-frame buildings.
- Plywood has excellent strength due to its construction; each layer is glued with the grain running 90° to the next.
- Ash has a 'springy' nature that makes it suitable for the handles of tools and sporting equipment.

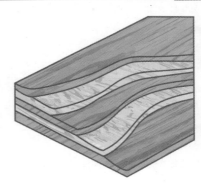

Figure 7.1 Plywood construction

Materials can be enhanced to resist and work with forces and stresses to improve functionality

Laminated beams can be glued together to form large arching supports for buildings.

Figure 7.2 Laminated timber beams above a Crossrail station in London

Exam practice answers at **www.hoddereducation.co.uk/6 myrevisionnotesdownloads**

Ecological and social footprint

Ecological issues in the design and manufacture of products

- If the felling of timber is not managed, then deforestation occurs.
- Deforestation can lead to fertile soil being washed away, leading to a barren landscape.
- Deforestation causes the loss of habitats for wildlife.
- The transportation of logs to a saw mill can be done by floating them down the river.
- When correctly managed, timber is an ecologically-sound material with a good social footprint.
- Young trees convert more carbon dioxide into oxygen than older trees do, therefore felling of old trees and replacing them with saplings has ecological benefits.
- The conversion of timber into planks requires a limited use of fossil fuels to power machinery.
- Timber is biodegradable and therefore has little effect on the environment if it goes to landfill.

The six Rs

- Reduce: We should reduce the use of manufactured boards as they are not as environmentally friendly as natural timbers, as many cannot be recycled.
- Reuse: Timber products can be reused, for example, old railway sleepers can be used to produce flower beds.
- Refuse: We should refuse to buy timber-based products that do not come from managed forests.
- Repair: Timber-based products are relatively easy to repair using glues if they become broken.
- Recycle: Most natural timbers are recyclable.
- Rethink: Manufacturers should rethink the use of manufactured boards.

Social issues in the design and manufacture of products

The owners of managed forests should:
- provide employment for workers
- ensure that workers are paid a fair wage
- ensure that workers are given the correct safety clothing and training.

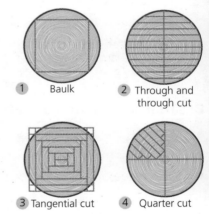

1 Baulk   2 Through and through cut

3 Tangential cut   4 Quarter cut

Figure 7.3 Conversion

Sources and origins

Conversion

- When a tree is **felled**, it contains a lot of moisture and is known as **green timber**.
- A felled tree is then **converted** into planks by one of four different methods.

Table 7.1 Conversion processes

Conversion process	Description	Common uses
Baulk cut	Simplest method: The trunk is cut into a square or rectangular section. This removes the bark and evens up the trunk.	Beams in the construction of timber-framed buildings
Through and through cut	Most popular method; simple and cost-effective. The trunk is sawn into planks. Can lead to a number of problems with warping and twisting. Most commonly used with softwoods.	Many areas of general joinery
Tangential cut	The trunk is cut tangentially to the circular trunk. This produces an attractive grain pattern and the wood is less likely to warp and twist. Used for both soft and hardwoods.	Where the natural attractiveness of the grain is important, such as during the manufacturing of furniture
Quarter cut	A complex method that produces a lot of waste. It is expensive financially and environmentally. The trunk is cut radially out from the centre. Generally used for expensive hardwoods.	To manufacture high quality furniture. Oak furniture will display 'figuring'; this shows up as silver markings that catch the light

Seasoning

- When converted into planks, timber must be **seasoned** to reduce its moisture content.
- Unseasoned timber is difficult to work and is vulnerable to rotting and insect attack.
- There are two methods of seasoning timber:
  - **Air seasoning**: Air is allowed to flow around the stacked timber and gradually dries out the timber. This process can take a number of years.
  - **Kiln seasoning**: The stack of timber is housed in a kiln where steam is allowed to flow around the timber. This is a quicker process.

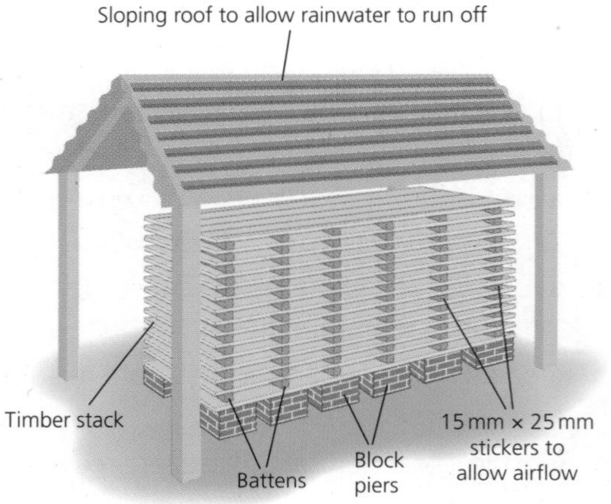

Creation of manufactured timbers

- Plywood is made by gluing layers (veneers) of wood together.
- Chipboard is made by gluing and pressing chips/flakes of wood together.
- MDF is made by gluing and pressing fibres of wood together.

Functionality: how well a material will fit its intended purpose.

Aesthetics: the style and appearance of a material.

Felling: the process of cutting down trees.

Green timber: timber that has just been felled and contains a lot of moisture.

Conversion: the process of cutting a log up into planks.

Seasoning: the process of removing moisture from newly-converted planks.

Sloping roof to allow rainwater to run off

Timber stack · Battens · Block piers · 15 mm × 25 mm stickers to allow airflow

Figure 7.4 Air seasoning

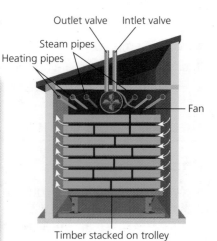

Outlet valve · Intlet valve · Steam pipes · Heating pipes · Fan · Timber stacked on trolley

Figure 7.5 Kiln seasoning

Using and working with timber-based materials

There are a range of specific marking out, cutting, shaping and joining methods used with timer-based materials and it is important to know which ones to use.

Marking out

- A pencil and a ruler are used to mark out wood.
- A try square will give you an accurate 90°-line to an edge. It will also allow you to check to see if an angle is at 90°.
- A template can be used as a method of marking out irregular shapes on wood. You can also draw around it to use it as an aid to quantity production.

Sawing wood

- A tenon saw will cut straight lines in wood. Make sure the wood is firmly held in a vice or with a G-clamp.
- A hand saw is used for cutting large pieces of wood and a coping saw will cut curves. The coping saw can be difficult to use accurately and therefore you should always cut slightly away from your line.

Figure 7.6 **Sawing with a tenon saw**

Shaping wood

- Wood can be easily shaped using a surform or wood rasp.
- A disc sander, belt sander and linisher are machines that use coarse glass paper to shape and smooth wood.
- Planes can be used to smooth and shape wood.
- There are a variety of different drills used for making holes in wood. A hole saw can produce large holes; a Forstner bit can produce flat bottom holes of varying sizes.
- Chisels are used to shape wood but are also very useful when cutting joints. Care should be taken when chiselling as chisels are very sharp. Always have your hands behind the cutting edge and securely clamp your work.

Joining wood

- There are a wide range of methods of joining wood and we categorise these into carcase, stool and frame joints.
- Carcase joints are used to make box-type constructions. Joints such as the 'butt joint' are quite simple to produce but are relatively weak. The 'dovetail joint' is difficult to produce but provides very good strength.
- Stools tables and chairs can be constructed using stool joints.

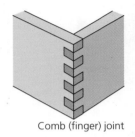

Comb (finger) joint

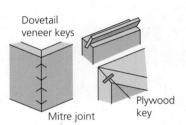

Dovetail veneer keys

Mitre joint

Plywood key

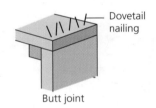

Dovetail nailing

Butt joint

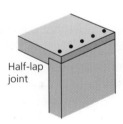

Half-lap joint

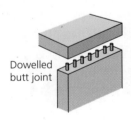

Dowelled butt joint

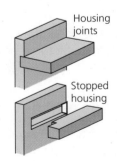

Housing joints

Stopped housing

Figure 7.7 **Carcase or box joints**

- Wooden windows and doors are produced using frame joints.
- The two most popular glues used when joining wood are PVA (polyvinyl acetate) and contact adhesive. PVA is a very strong glue but it takes quite a long time to dry. Contact adhesive is a medium strength glue but, as the name suggests, it provides a quick joint.

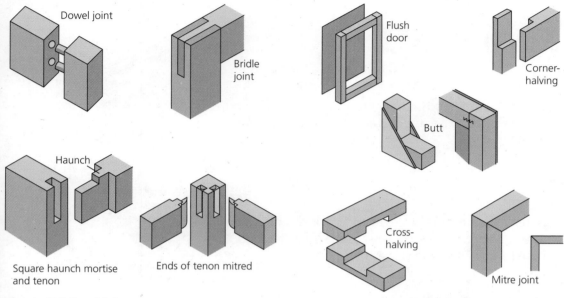

Dowel joint

Bridle joint

Haunch

Square haunch mortise and tenon

Ends of tenon mitred

Figure 7.8 Stool joints

Flush door

Corner-halving

Butt

Cross-halving

Mitre joint

Figure 7.9 Frame joints

Stock forms, types and sizes

It is important to know the common stock forms of timber as this will assist you when designing and making products using wood.

Natural timber

- Natural timber that has come straight from the saw mill is known a **rough sawn**.
- It is generally used for construction work where appearance is not important.
- Timber that has had just its sides planed is known as **planed both sides (PBS)**.
- Timber that has had all sides planed is known as **planed square edge (PSE)** or **planed all round (PAR)**.
- PSE can be used for a wide variety of applications including interior joinery.

> **Rough sawn**: timber straight from the saw.
>
> **PBS (planed both sides)**: timber that has had two sides planed.
>
> **PAR (planed all round) / PSE (planed square edge)**: timber that has all sides planed.

Manufactured boards

- Manufactured boards such as medium density fibreboard (MDF), plywood and chipboard come in large sheets: 2400 x 1200 mm.
- Did you know that the size of the original transit van was based on the size of a manufactured board!
- Plywood can range in thickness from 1 mm to up to 25 mm.

Mouldings and dowelling

- Timber can also be supplied in a wide range of decorative mouldings.
- These are very useful when producing products such as picture frames.
- Dowelling is timber that is cylindrical and is useful for making wooden rails.

Figure 7.10 Mouldings

Exam practice answers at www.hoddereducation.co.uk/6 myrevisionnotesdownloads

Timber-based components

Woodscrews

- Woodscrews are a quick and convenient method of fastening two or more components together.
- Modern woodscrews are made from steel but have a protective coating to stop them from rusting.
- They are designed to be used with power tools such as a cordless drill for fast fixing.

Hinges

- Hinges are used to allow wooden parts to swing, for example doors and lids.
- There are a variety of different types of hinge that are used in different applications.

> **KD (knock down) fittings:** commercially-made fittings general used with self-assembly furniture.

Table 7.2 Common hinges

Butt hinge		Probably the most widely-used hinge
		For examples: jewellery boxes (a small pair made from brass), a house door (a large pair made from low-carbon steel or stainless steel)
		Where a door is heavy, such as a front door or fire door, the butt hinges are likely to have ball bearings between the parts to help spread the load of the door
		Usually recessed into wooden surfaces
		Need to be very precisely aligned
Concealed hinge		For example, kitchen cabinet doors
		Usually sprung so that they self close
		Often a soft-close device is included, so that the doors do not slam shut
		Easy to adjust to help with alignment of the doors
Piano hinge		This is like a butt hinge, but comes in one long length, which you cut to size
		Lids that covers the keys on a traditional piano (it gets its name from its common use)
Flush hinge		These are fitted between a door and a frame, like a butt hinge, but are not usually recessed
		Because they are not recessed, they are easier to fit, but look less attractive

KD fittings

- **Knock-down (KD) fittings** are often used with 'flat-pack furniture'.
- They enable furniture to be sold unassembled, taken home in a flat cardboard box and assembled using simple tools.
- The concept of flat-pack furniture has greatly reduced the cost of buying furniture.
- Traditionally, a family would invest in a piece of furniture which would then be handed down through the generations. Now people can afford to replace furniture as fashion and style changes.

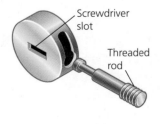
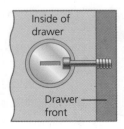

Figure 7.11 Camlock fitting

Scales of production

There are four main scales of production:

- Prototype – this is an early example of a product that is produced as a 'one off' to test the concept or the process. A prototype can also be a bespoke product made for a particular purpose. An example of prototype timber-based products could include handmade furniture.
- Batch production – this involves producing a limited range of products. It usually involves the use of machinery. An example of timber-based batch production could include the production of hardwood garden furniture.
- Mass production – this is where large quantities of identical products are made and will almost certainly involve machinery. An example of timber-based mass production could include the manufacture of kitchen cupboard doors.
- Continuous production – involves the constant manufacture of products and would normally be carried out using fully-automated machinery. An example of timber-based continuous production could include the manufacture of flat-pack furniture.

Figure 7.12 A mitre square

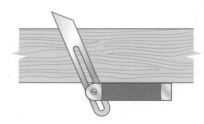

Figure 7.13 A sliding bevel

Specialist techniques and processes

The use of production aids

There are many tools and devices that can speed up and increase the accuracy and consistency of production.

- A steel tape measure can be used to measure lengths of between 5 and 20 metres.
- A try square enables you to mark out or check a 90° angle.
- A mitre square will allow you to mark out or check a 45° angle.
- A sliding bevel can be set at any angle.
- A marking gauge marks a line parallel to an edge, while a mortise gauge will mark a double line parallel to an edge.
- **Templates** are often used to mark irregular shapes on wood.
- A **jig** is a specially made device designed to help in the production of a component.

Figure 7.14 A marking gauge

Tools, equipment and processes

There are a number of specialist wood tools that can be used when working timber-based materials.

- A scroll saw – is a mechanised version of the coping saw. It will speed up the cutting process and increases the accuracy of the cut.
- A jigsaw – can be fitted with a range of different types of blade to enable it to cut different types of wood of a variety of thicknesses. It is particularly useful for cutting large manufactured boards.
- Chisels – there are three types of chisel that can be used to cut and shape wood:
  - A firmer chisel is a general-purpose chisel that can be used for a wide range of processes.
  - A bevel–edge chisel can be used to clean acute-angle corners such as when cleaning up a dovetail joint.
  - A mortise chisel is a strengthened chisel that can be used with a mallet when cutting out a mortise hole.

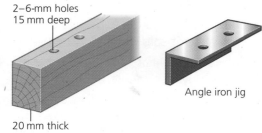

Figure 7.15 A mortise gauge

2–6-mm holes
15 mm deep

20 mm thick

Angle iron jig

Figure 7.16 A drilling jig

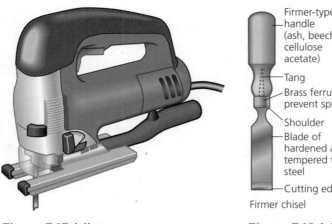

Figure 7.17 A jigsaw

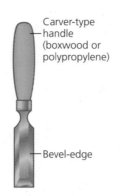

Firmer-type handle (ash, beech or cellulose acetate)

Tang

Brass ferrule to prevent splitting

Shoulder

Blade of hardened and tempered tool steel

Cutting edge

Firmer chisel

Figure 7.18 A firmer chisel

Carver-type handle (boxwood or polypropylene)

Bevel-edge

Figure 7.19 A bevel-edge chisel

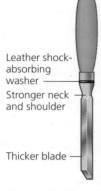

Leather shock-absorbing washer

Stronger neck and shoulder

Thicker blade

Figure 7.20 A mortise chisel

How materials are cut, shaped and formed to a tolerance

- Timber-based materials are cut, shaped and formed to a tolerance.
- This means that they are not expected to be made to an exact measurement but are to be made to within a tolerance. For example, a table top that is to be made 1000 mm long could be given a tolerance of plus or minus one millimetre. This means that the size could be anything between 999 mm and 1001 mm.
- Natural timber is hydroscopic. This means that it absorbs moisture, which will make it swell, or it can dry out, which will make it shrink. By seasoning timber to a specific level of moisture content we can minimise this amount of dimensional change.

Commercial processes

Routing

- Hand-held routers can be used to cut grooves and channels in wood. They can also produce decorative edges.
- In industry, routers can be mounted under a table to increase their versatility.
- CNC routers will follow CAD drawings to accurately and consistently produce identical wooden components.

Forming

- Bends and curves can be formed into wood by a number of processes.
- Kerfing is a simple method of producing a bend in wood by sawing a series of cuts partway through the wood, allowing it to bend. Once glued, the wood will stay in this shape.

> **Template**: a two-dimensional profile of an object that is to be cut.
>
> **Jig**: a three-dimensional aid to a production process.

Figure 7.21 CNC wood router

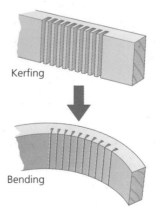

Kerfing

Bending

Figure 7.22 Kerfing

The application and use of quality control to include measurable and quantitative systems used during manufacture

Quality control checks are made to assess the quality of wooden products as they are being made:

- Wood should be initially checked for any defects such as warping, twisting, cupping or bowing.
- The moisture content of wood should be checked to ensure its suitability for the environment it is to be used in.
- Regular measurements should be taken to ensure that the product is being made to the correct size.
- Visual checks should be made to see if the surface is smooth and free from any unwanted marks.
- The use of templates, moulds, formers, fences and depth-stops and the use of CNC equipment will help increase the accuracy and consistency of a product.

> **Quality control**: checks made during manufacture to ensure accuracy is maintained.

Surface treatment and finishes

REVISED

Timber-based products are often given a surface treatment to alter their appearance or protect them from external elements such as the weather.

Surface preparation

- Scratches, dents and unwanted marks should first be removed from the surface of the wood by planing and/or sanding with glass paper.
- Glass paper is graded from rough to fine and you should work your way through the grades to achieve the correct level of smoothness.
- A disc sander, palm sander, belt sander and linisher are all mechanised sanding machines that can speed up the process.
- The surface should then be cleared of any dust, oil or grease before a finish is applied.

Painting

- Paints are generally used to change the colour of the wood and the natural grain of the wood is normally then hidden.
- Surface preparation of the wood is essential.
- A section of pine that contains knots would need to:
  - be sanded smooth
  - have a knotting compound applied to the knots
  - receive a primer coat, then an undercoat and then a gloss coat.
- At each stage the surface would need to be sanded smooth.

Varnishing

- Varnishes can be clear or combined with a wood stain.
- They can provide a gloss, satin or matt finish.
- Polyurethane-based varnishes provide good outdoor protection.
- Water-based acrylic varnishes are environmentally friendly and tend to be for inside use.

Exam practice answers at www.hoddereducation.co.uk/6 myrevisionnotesdownloads

Tanilising

- Tanilising is a commercial process of pressure-treating timber with a preservative.
- Timber is placed in a special chamber where preservatives are forced into the cells of the timber under pressure.
- Tanilised timber is used where a high resistance to decay is needed.
- Typical uses include patio decking and garden sheds.

Exam tip

If the question asks for detailed notes and sketches of a process, make sure that you provide a series of correctly-sequenced labelled diagrams, add a detailed commentary and be sure to use the correct technical terminology.

Typical mistake

Make sure you don't leave out vital information when answering a question that requires details of a process.

For example, when asked to 'describe in detail how you would prepare and apply a finish to teak patio furniture', don't miss the preparation stage and therefore lose valuable marks.

Make sure you plan your answer before diving in.

Now test yourself

TESTED

1 Name a suitable timber for use as a garden bench and explain your choice.   [3 marks]
2 Use notes and sketches to describe how to air season newly-converted timber.   [6 marks]
3 Explain the advantages of using KD fittings.   [4 marks]
4 Use notes and sketches to describe how to produce a bend in wood using the kerfing technique. [6 marks]
5 Give two reasons why it is necessary to apply a finish to a wooden external door.   [2 marks]

8 Metal-based materials

In the exam you will only need to answer questions on this content in relation to one material category or system. You only need to revise this topic if you plan to answer questions with a focus on metal-based materials.

Selection of materials and components

Different types of metal have quite different characteristics. It is essential to have a knowledge of their working properties so that you can match the metal to its intended purpose.

Figure 8.1 Copper piping

Functionality

- An aeroplane needs to be both lightweight and strong; this makes aluminium the most obvious choice.
- Kitchen knives need to be strong, corrosion-resistant and able to hold a sharp edge. This makes stainless steel the most suitable metal.
- Copper is a corrosion-resistant metal that is ductile and can be easily joined, making it the most popular metal for use in domestic plumbing.

Aesthetics

- Gold is considered to be an attractive metal due to its warm colouring.
- Many metals, such as stainless steel and aluminium, can be polished to a mirror-like finish.

Environmental factors

- Metals come from **ore** which is non-renewable. The processing of **turning** ore into pure metal uses a lot of energy. Most of this energy comes from non-renewable fossil fuels.
- Some metals will pollute the ground if they go to landfill.
- Most metals are relatively easily to repair, have a good lifespan and can be recycled.

Figure 8.2 Aluminium drinks cans can be recycled

Availability

- There is a limited supply of metal ore in the Earth's crust and therefore it will not always be available.
- Metal comes in stock sizes of length, width, thickness (gauge), diameter and weight.

Cost

- The cost of metals can vary quite considerably. Common metals such as steel are relatively inexpensive. Semi-precious metals such as copper, tin and lead are more expensive, while precious metals such as gold and silver are very expensive.
- Metals are suitable for batch, mass and continuous methods of manufacture, which reduces the unit cost of metal products.
- Bulk buying of metals can reduce the cost of the material.

Social and cultural factors

- Metals used for construction, such as steel, are very accessible and affordable, therefore they are extensively used for a variety of products.
- Precious metals such as gold and silver are only affordable to the wealthier members of society.

Ethical factors

- Metals are a finite resource and must be recycled or they will not be available for future generations.
- The processing of metal ore pollutes the planet.

Forces and stresses

REVISED ☐

Forces and stresses act upon metal due to external factors. For example, a chair undergoes stress when someone sits on it. Stresses can be categorised into four types.

- Tension: this is when a force is attempting to pull something apart. Think of the forces applied to a rope during a tug of war.
- Compression: this is when a force is attempting to squash something. Think of the leg of a table.
- Bending: this happens when a force is trying to bend something. Think of what happens when too many books are placed on a shelf – it begins to sag in the middle.
- Torsion: this occurs when a force is trying to twist something. Think of the force required to unscrew a bottle top.

Figure 8.3 Millau suspension bridge

Materials and objects can be manipulated to resist and work with forces and stresses

Most metals can withstand an impressive amount of force and stress.

- Steel is an excellent construction material as it has great strength.
- It has exceptional tensile strength and this allows steel cables to be used to hold up suspension bridges.
- Softer metals such as lead are malleable and can withstand being beaten into shape without cracking.
- Have a look at where a chimney enters the roof of a house. The silver metal around the chimney is made from lead and has been beaten into shape.
- Copper is a ductile metal and can withstand being drawn out into fine wire.
- The metal inside most of the electrical cables in your house is copper.

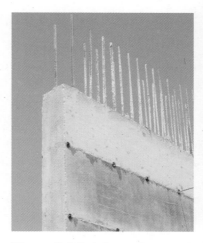

Figure 8.4 Reinforced concrete

Materials can be enhanced to resist and work with forces and stresses to improve functionality

Metals can be used to enhance the functionality of different materials.

- Steel rods can be used to improve the strength of concrete.
- Sheet metal can be corrugated to provide extra strength.

Figure 8.5 Corrugated steel

Ecological and social footprint

Ecological issues in the design and manufacture of products

Metal has both positive and negative impacts on the ecology and society.

- The mining and processing of metal ores creates employment for many people in countries all over the world.
- The mining of metal ore can create scars on the landscape and have a negative effect on the habitat of wildlife.
- Metal products are generally non-biodegradable and some can even pollute the ground.
- Metal products can be repaired and recycled.

Figure 8.6 Mining metal ore

The six Rs

- Reduce: Manufacturers of metal products should reduce the amount of new metal used and increase the amount of recycled metal.
- Reuse: Metal-based products can be reused, for example old gold rings can be reworked into new items of jewellery.
- Refuse: We should refuse to buy metal-based products that are toxic to the environment, such as lead.
- Repair: Metal-based products can be glued or welded if they become broken.
- Recycle: Nearly all metal can be recycled.
- Rethink: Manufacturers should rethink the use of toxic metals and the use of new metal.

Social issues in the design and manufacture of products

- Employers in the metal-based manufacturing industry should ensure that workers are looked after by:
  - ensuring that they have safe working conditions as manufacturing in metal can be a very hazardous environment
  - ensuring that workers are paid a living wage.
- The extraction of metal ore from the land by opencast mining can produce scars on the landscape.
- The processing of metal from its ore produces atmospheric pollution by releasing sulphur dioxide, leading to poor air quality.

Sources and origins

As responsible designers, it is important that we understand the journey that the metals have undertaken before we use them.

- Metals are found in the Earth's crust and are embedded in rock known as ore.
- Ore can be opencast mined, underground mined or even dredged from rivers.
- Iron comes from an ore called **haematite** which can be found in countries such as Brazil, Australia and Africa.
- Ore must be **smelted** to release the metal from the rock.
- Iron is extracted from haematite by a process called smelting. This involves heating the ore to a very high temperature in a blast furnace.

Figure 8.7 Mining haematite

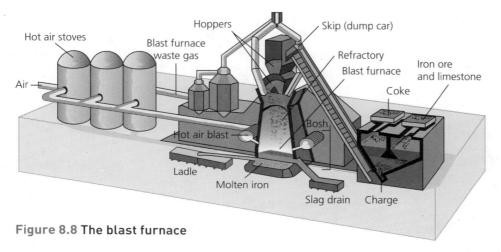

Figure 8.8 The blast furnace

- Aluminium comes from an ore known as **bauxite** which can be found in countries such as Australia and Guinea.
- Aluminium is extracted from bauxite by an electrolytic process.
- The electrolytic process takes place in a reduction cell.
- In a reduction cell a very high current of electricity is used to extract the aluminium from its ore.

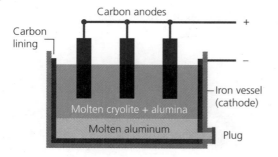

Figure 8.9 The reduction cell

Ore: rock which contains metal.

Turning: a method of producing cylinders and cones using a centre lathe.

Haematite: ore containing iron.

Smelting: the process of extracting metal from ore.

Bauxite: ore containing aluminium.

Using and working with metal-based materials

Properties of materials

See Tables 6.6 and 6.7 (page 20) for properties of metals.

The modification of properties for specific purposes

Metals can be combined to improve their performance for specific purposes.

- Copper can be alloyed with zinc to produce brass. This is a much stronger metal.
- Chromium can be added to steel to make stainless steel, a much harder and corrosion-resistant metal.

Metals can be heat-treated to improve their performance.

- Steel can be hardened by heating to red hot and quickly quenching it.
- Metals can be softened by heating and cooling them very slowly. This makes them malleable and reduces any work hardening. Work hardening occurs when metal is subjected to strain, for example when it is continually bent forwards and backwards or beaten with a hammer.

How to shape and form using cutting, abrasion and addition

You can read about techniques to shape and form metal in the section on techniques and processes on page 44.

Stock forms, types and sizes

It is important to consider the common stock forms and sizes of metal when designing and making metal components. This will save you time and effort as metal is a hard material to cut and shape.

- Sheet metal is available in a variety of thicknesses, known as 'standard wire gauge' (SWG), and a range of sheet sizes.
- Rod, bar, and tube are extrusions that are available in a range of diameters and cross-sectional sizes and a variety of long lengths.

Components

- Rivets provide a permanent mechanical fixing for metal components.
- Machine screws allow metal components to be non-permanently fixed together.
- Nuts, bolts and washers are the most common method of non-permanently fixing metal components together.

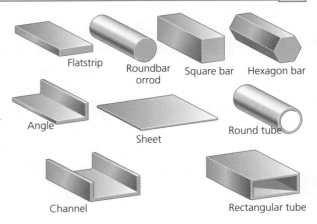

Figure 8.10 Standard stock forms of metal

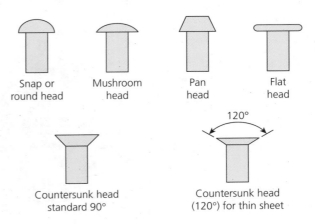

Figure 8.11 Types of rivet

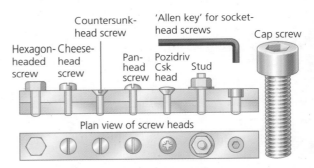

Figure 8.12 Types of machine screw

Figure 8.13 Nut, bolt and washer

Scales of production

There are four main scales of production.

- Prototype – this is an early example of a product that is produced as a 'one off' to test the concept or the process. A prototype can also be a bespoke product made for a particular purpose. An example of prototype metal-based products could include a casting of a church bell.
- Batch production – this involves producing a limited range of products. It usually involves the use of machinery. An example of metal-based batch production could include the production of mountain bike frames.
- Mass production – this is where large quantities of identical products are made and will almost certainly involve machinery. An example of metal-based mass production could include the manufacture of cars.
- Continuous production – involves the constant manufacture of products and would normally be carried out using fully-automated machinery. An example of metal-based continuous production could include the manufacture of aluminium drinks cans.

Specialist techniques and processes

Using production aids

The accuracy and consistency of production can be improved by the use of a range of specific tools and equipment.

- A scriber will act as pencil on metal, layout fluid makes it easier to mark out on shiny metal and an engineer's square will produce an accurate 90° line.
- Calipers can be used to measure the inside diameter of a hole and the outside of a metal bar. Odd-leg calipers will produce a parallel line to an edge.

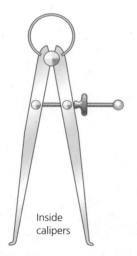

Inside calipers

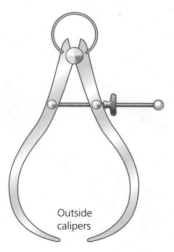

Outside calipers

Figure 8.14 A pair of inside calipers   **Figure 8.15 A pair of outside calipers**

- A digital micrometre and a digital vernier caliper can measure to an accuracy of 100th of a millimetre. That's 0.01 mm.

Tools, equipment and processes

There are a range of specific marking-out, cutting, shaping and joining methods used with metal-based materials, and it is important to know which ones to use.

Marking out

- A scriber acts as a pencil when marking out on metal. On bright metal, it is useful to use layout fluid to make it easier to see the lines.
- An engineer's square produces a 90° line to an edge, and a centre punch will mark the centre of a hole before drilling.

Sawing

- The hacksaw is the most common saw used for cutting straight lines in metal. A junior hacksaw is a small version used for cutting smaller metal parts.
- Bandsaws, jigsaws and even a coping saw can all be fitted with metal cutting blades.

Shaping

- Metal can be shaped using a range of different shaped files.
- Files are graded depending on their roughness: these are known as 'rough cut', 'second cut' and 'smooth cut'.

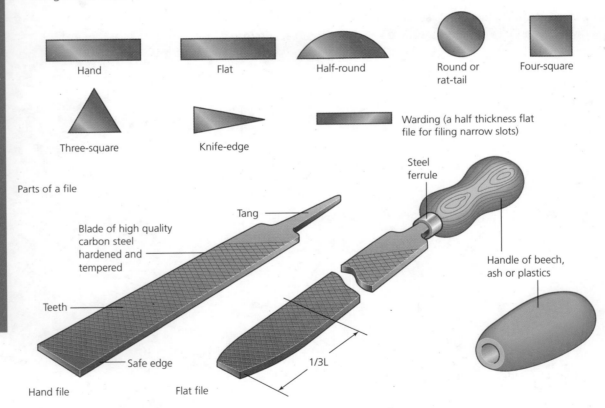

Figure 8.16 **Different types of file**

- **Cross filing** is an effective method of shaping metal.
- You should use the full length of the file and remember that the file only cuts on the forward stock.

Cross filing: a method of shaping metal using files.

Draw filing: a method of smoothing the edges of metal.

Figure 8.17 Cross filing

- **Draw filing** smooths the edges of metal.
- Place the file across the edge of the metal while holding the blade rather than the handle. Then move the file forwards and backwards to achieve a flat, smooth edge.

Figure 8.18 Draw filing

Joining

- Metal can be joined in a number of non-permanent ways, such as with nuts and bolts, and self-tapping screws.
- Metal can be permanently joined by soldering and welding.
- Soft soldering can be used when attaching copper pipe fittings together.
- The joint is first cleaned, a paste flux is applied, and then it is heated with a torch. The solder then melts and flows into the joint.
- Solder that is to be used for plumbing is made from tin and copper.
- Hard soldering is a similar method to soft soldering but is used for joining precious metals such as gold and silver.
- Brazing uses brass as solder to attach steel components together.
- Welding uses heat to melt the surface of a metal. Once the metal is in a molten state, it 'pools' together and any gaps are filled with a filler rod.

Riveting

- Riveting is a mechanical method of permanently fixing metal parts together.
- A hole is drilled through the metal components.
- A rivet is then placed in the hole and hammered into shape. When pop riveting, a rivet gun is used to form the rivet.

How materials are cut, shaped and formed to a tolerance

Metal is a much harder and more stable material than wood or polymers and therefore it can be cut and machined to much finer **tolerances**.

- Tolerances are normally expressed as a maximum and minimum size.
- For example: a 25 mm diameter would be expressed as '25 +/− 0.02'.
- This means the maximum size the diameter could be is 25.02 mm and the minimum size would be 24.98 mm.

Figure 8.19 **Soldering copper piping**

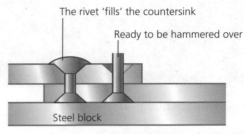

The rivet 'fills' the countersink

Ready to be hammered over

Steel block

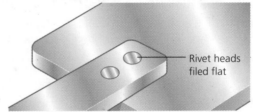

Rivet heads filed flat

Figure 8.20 **The riveting process**

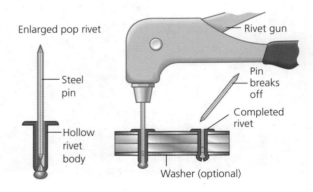

Enlarged pop rivet

Rivet gun

Steel pin

Pin breaks off

Completed rivet

Hollow rivet body

Washer (optional)

Figure 8.21 **Pop riveting**

> **Tolerance**: the acceptable difference between the upper and lower sizes of a metal component.

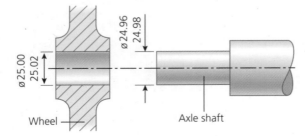

Wheel

Axle shaft

Figure 8.22 **Tolerance**

Commercial processes

There are a number of metal-specific tools, equipment and processes that can speed up production and improve both the accuracy and consistency of your work.

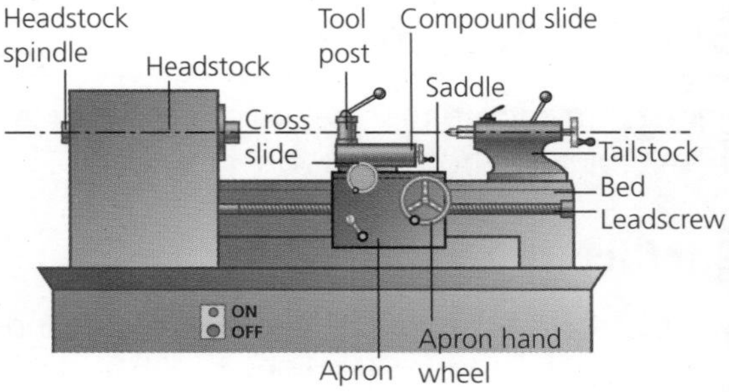

Milling

Milling machines will machine flat surfaces and allow slots and grooves to be cut into metal.

Casting

Casting involves pouring molten metal into a pre-prepared mould.

Pewter casting

Pewter casting involves casting pewter into a pre-prepared mould.

- A mould is designed on a CAD program such as 2D Design.
- The mould can then be cut from medium density fibreboard (MDF) using a laser cutter.
- If CAD/CAM is not available, then use a paper template and cut the mould from MDF using a coping saw.
- Pewter (90 per cent tin and 10 per cent copper) is heated to a molten state (200°C).
- The pewter is then poured into the mould and allowed to cool.

Sand casting

Sand casting involves casting high-temperature-melting metals such as aluminium and iron into a pre-prepared sand mould.

- A pattern is first produced from close-grained hardwood such a jelutong, or from a moulding-foam polymer.
- The pattern is then used to produce a mould in sand.
- The aluminium is then heated to a molten state (660°).
- The aluminium is then poured into the mould and allowed to cool.

The application and use of quality control to include measurable and quantitative systems used during manufacture

Quality control checks on metal components can be done using some sophisticated equipment.

- A **go-no-go gauge** is used to check that a measurement is within tolerance.
- A **depth-stop** can be used on a drilling machine to ensure that a hole is drilled to the correct depth.
- A metal rule can be used to ensure that the product is being made to the correct size.
- Visual checks should be made to see that the surface is smooth and free from any unwanted marks.
- The use of templates, moulds, formers, fences, and CNC equipment will help increase the accuracy and consistency of a metal product.

Figure 8.23 Lathe operations

Headstock spindle
Headstock
Tool post
Compound slide
Saddle
Cross slide
Tailstock
Bed
Leadscrew
ON OFF
Apron hand wheel
Apron

Figure 8.24 Metal-cutting chop saw using an end stop

Milling: cutting grooves and slots into metal.

Casting: a method of heating metal into a molten state and pouting it into a pre-prepared mould.

Go-no-go gauge: a special tool that checks the size of a metal component.

Depth-stop: a mechanical means of setting how deep a drill bit will cut, used for quality control.

Surface treatment and finishes

Finishes are applied to metals to change their appearance and/or to give them protection from corrosion.

Surface preparation

- Metal surfaces should be free from marks and scratches. This can be achieved by rubbing then down with abrasive cloths such as emery cloth or 'wet or dry' paper.
- Abrasive cloths/papers are graded depending on their coarseness.
- The higher the number, the smoother the grade; 80 grit is a rough paper while 400 grit is smooth.
- The surface should then be cleaned of any dust, oil or grease before a finish is applied.

Dip coating

- Dip coating covers the metal in a layer of polyethylene.
- The metal is fully cleaned and then placed into an oven and heated to a temperature of 200°C.
- The metal is then dipped into a fluidising bath for a few seconds.
- The polyethylene sticks and melts onto the hot surface leaving a smooth, shiny coating.

Powder coating

- This is an industrial equivalent of dip coating.
- The metal is fully cleaned and then placed into an oven and heated to a temperature of 200°C.
- The metal is then sprayed with a layer of powdered polyethylene from an electrostatic spray gun.
- The electrostatic spray gun ensures an even coating over the metal.
- The metal is then placed back into the oven to cure.

Galvanising

- This is an industrial process that involves coating the metal in zinc.
- The metal is fully cleaned and then dipped into a bath of molten zinc.
- The zinc provides a very durable and corrosion-resistant barrier.

Figure 8.25 Powder coating

Figure 8.26 Galvanised steel safety barrier beside a road

Now test yourself

TESTED

1. Use notes and sketches to describe the life cycle of an aluminium can. [6 marks]
2. Name two methods of permanently joining metal together. [2 marks]
3. Name two non-permanent methods of joining metal together. [2 marks]
4. Explain what is meant by the term 'tolerance' when machining metal. [2 marks]
5. Use notes and sketches to describe how to powder coat metal. [6 marks]

Exam practice answers at **www.hoddereducation.co.uk/6 myrevisionnotesdownloads**

9 Polymers

In the exam you will only need to answer questions on this content in relation to one material category or system. You only need to revise this topic if you plan to answer questions with a focus on polymers.

Selection of materials and components

Polymers have quite different characteristics from timber or metal-based materials. Understanding polymers will help you to increase the creativity and originality in the shape of your designs.

Functionality

- Polymers are naturally waterproof, which makes them ideally suited for use as liquid containers such as drinks bottles.
- Illuminated shop signs use the transparent and translucent qualities of polymers to draw attention to and advertise the shop.
- The mouldability of polymers is used to produce ergonomic designs, such as that of a video games controller.

Figure 9.1 A moulded polymer bucket and spade

Aesthetics

- A colour pigment can be added to polymers to alter its colour. Children's toys are normally brightly coloured to attract their attention.
- The surface finish of a polymer can be altered during the moulding process.
- Your smartphone will have a very smooth, highly polished surface. The school chair that you are sitting on will probably have a textured surface to stop you slipping off.
- The moulding process allows flowing, curved, polymer shapes to be produced.

Environmental factors

- Polymers come from crude oil which is a non-renewable fossil fuel. The processing of crude oil into a polymer uses a lot of energy and creates pollution.
- Most polymers are non-biodegradable and if they go to landfill they will last for many, many years. Polymers that find their way into the oceans are being ingested by fish and are finding their way back into the food chain.
- Polymers are not easy to repair but they are durable and can have a good lifespan. Many polymers can be recycled.
- **Biopolymers** are sourced from plants and are therefore renewable.

> **Biopolymers**: polymers which are made from plant material such as corn starch.

Availability

- There is only a limited amount of crude oil on the planet and therefore it will not always be available.
- Polymers come in a number of stock forms including sheet, tubing, rod, powder and granules, which are essential to the moulding processes.

Cost

- Polymer-based materials have undergone several processes before you get the material to work with. This makes the initial cost of polymers expensive when compared to most timber and metal-based materials.
- The suitability of polymers for quantity production reduces the overall cost of the polymer-based products when they are made in large quantities.
- The pen you are probably holding in your hand now is made from expensive polymers, but due to the highly-mechanised manufacturing process it is easily affordable.
- Bulk buying of polymers can reduce the cost of the material.

Social and cultural factors

- The development of inexpensive polymer-based products has led to a 'throwaway society'. This is one in which we discard products when they break because it is cheaper than having them repaired.
- The plastic shopping bag is an example of how people and governments are changing their attitude to the 'throwaway' society. More people now understand the negative effects of disposing of polymer-based products and are now reusing bags. Governments are legislating against throwaway bags by imposing charges.

Ethical factors

- Polymer-based products use up natural resources that will not be available for future generations.
- The disposal of polymer-based products can pollute the environment and harm both humans and wildlife.

Forces and stresses REVISED

Monomers are combined to produce polymers with quite different strength properties.

Materials and objects can be manipulated to resist and work with forces and stresses

- Acrylic (PMMA) is a brittle material with poor bending strength. Therefore, you would not want to use it where it had to withstand a load.
- ABS is very similar to acrylic but has good strength and impact resistance. Car indicator lenses and children toys are made from ABS.
- Glass reinforced plastic (GRP) has excellent strength and can be moulded to form the body of boat hulls.
- Carbon-fibre reinforced plastic (CFRP) has excellent strength and is relatively light in weight and is used to produce the body panels of Formula One racing cars.

Exam practice answers at www.hoddereducation.co.uk/6 myrevisionnotesdownloads

Materials can be enhanced to resist and work with forces and stresses to improve functionality

The inherent mouldabilty of polymers makes it relatively easy to introduce strengthening ribs and shapes into the design of a product.

● Plastic cups are moulded with ribs around the sides to make the very thin polymer sheet stronger.

Figure 9.2 Plastic cups

Ecological and social footprint

REVISED

Polymers can cause considerable ecological harm if they are not sourced, processed, used and disposed of in a responsible manner.

Ecological issues in the design and manufacture of products

● Drilling for oil can lead to spillages which have a disastrous effect on the environment and wildlife in the area.
● The **refining** of oil into polymers creates atmospheric pollution that can harm the air quality and contribute to global warming.

The six Rs

● Reduce: Manufacturers of polymer products should increase the amount of recycled polymer used and rely less on new material which uses the finite oil resource.
● Reuse: Polymer-based products can be reused, for example, margarine tubs can be used as storage boxes.
● Refuse: We can refuse to buy products that use unnecessary polymer packaging.
● Repair: Polymer-based products can be glued or welded if they become broken.
● Recycle: Nearly all thermoforming polymers can be recycled.
● Rethink: We can rethink how we use disposable polymer-based products such as disposable cutlery, razors and food packaging.

Social issues in the design and manufacture of products

● The extraction and refining of oil from the ground creates employment for people in many countries around the world.
● The relatively cheap cost of polymer-based products enables more people to buy new products that can improve the quality of their lives.
● However, this can contribute to a materialistic society where people feel pressured into having the latest products.
● There are many cases where the drilling and transportation of oil has led to accidents that have allowed oil to contaminate the land and harm wildlife.
● The refining of oil into polymers creates toxic gases that contribute to global warming.
● Most polymers are generally not biodegradable and some can even pollute the ground if not disposed of in a sensitive way.
● Thermoforming polymers can be recycled but thermosetting polymers are very difficult to reuse.

Figure 9.3 The impact of an oil spill on wildlife

> **Exam tip**
>
> Make sure that you know the difference between a thermoforming polymer and a thermosetting polymer.

Sources and origins

The majority of polymers come from crude oil, which is found throughout the world. The biggest deposits of crude oil are in the Middle East and in Central and South America.

- Crude oil is extracted from the ground by drilling and pumping it to the surface. It is then transported to an oil refinery to be processed.

There are three distinct stages to the processing of crude oil.

Stage 1: Fractional distillation

- Crude oil is boiled to produce gas.
- The gas is then vented off through a tall column where it condenses to form different petrochemical products such as gas, petrol and oil.
- The petrochemical used to produce polymers is called naphtha.

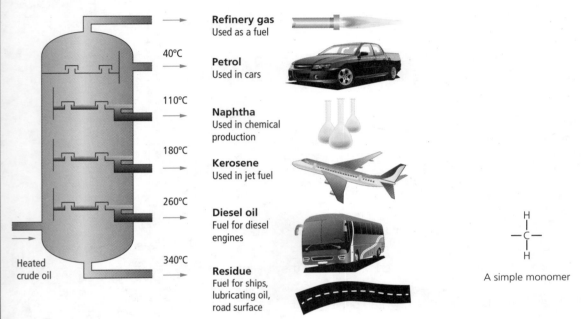

Figure 9.4 Fractional distillation

Stage 2: Cracking

- The naphtha is heated and condensed once again to break it down into the vital building blocks that are needed to produce polymers.
- The three main building blocks are ethylene, propylene and butylene.

A simple monomer

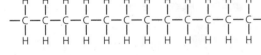

The structure of the polymer polyethylene

Figure 9.5 Monomers and polymers

Stage 3: Polymerisation

In the process of **polymerisation**, **monomers** are linked together to form polymers.

The monomer ethylene is linked to form polyethylene (PE), and propylene is linked together to form polypropylene (PP).

Refining: the processing of crude oil.

Fractional distillation: the process of separating crude oil into its different parts.

Polymerisation: joining monomers together to form polymers.

Monomers: the individual building blocks used to create polymers.

Using and working with polymer materials

The modification of properties for specific purposes

- Polymers can be modified to enhance their properties for a specific purpose.
- Stabilisers can be added to PVC to prevent UV degradation. An example of this is in window frames.
- See Tables 6.9 and 6.10 in Chapter 6 (page 22) for more on the properties of polymers.

Table 9.01 Methods of modifying polymers

Cutting	Polymers can be cut using a wide variety of metal and wood working tools.
	The laser cutter is an excellent method of cutting some polymers such as acrylic.
Drilling	Polymers can be drilled with regular drill bits.
	Placing masking tape over the surface will prevent the drill from slipping.
Casting	Thermosetting polymers such as polyester resin can be used to cast polymer shapes into a pre-prepared silicon mould.
Deforming	Thermoforming polymers can be heated and deformed into different shapes by line bending, vacuum forming, and variety of other industrial processes including injection and blow-moulding techniques.
Printing	Thermoforming polymers can be printed by the 3D printing processes. The 3D printer will layer powdered or a filament of polymer following a 3D CAD image.
Joining	Polymers can be joined in a wide variety of permanent and non-permanent ways.
	Nuts, bolts and washers are an effective method of joining polymers.
	Pop rivets can be used to join sheet polymers.
	Solvent-based adhesives such as Tensol cement will weld the surfaces of polymers together forming a permanent joint.

Stock forms, types and sizes

Polymer is available in a wide range of forms, colours and thicknesses. A big advantage of using polymers is that they can be bought self-coloured with an immaculate high gloss finish.

Table 9.2 Polymer stock forms

Stock form	Description
Sheet	The most commonly used sheet polymer in the school workshop is acrylic (PMMA). The sheets come in regular sizes measuring 1200 x 600 x 3 mm.
	Other polymer sheet materials include high impact polystyrene (HIPS). This is available in a size that fits most vacuum forming machines: 475 x 274 x 1 mm
Rod	This comes in a range of diameters and is particularly useful for transmitting light.
Powder	Used in the fluidising bath as part of the plastic-dipping process. In industry it would be used in powder coating and also used with thermosetting polymers in compression moulding.
Granules	Mainly used in industrial processes such as injection moulding and extrusion.
Foams	Available in large sheets (1200 x 600 mm) and extensively used in schools for model making.
Films	A very thin sheet that is usually sold in rolls.

Figure 9.6 Acrylic (PMMA) sheet

Figure 9.7 Polymer extrusions

- There are a number of **pre-manufactured polymer components** that are available. These include items such as nuts, bolts, hinges and shelf brackets.

Figure 9.8 Granulated polymer

Figure 9.9 PVC film

Figure 9.10 Polymer hinge

Figure 9.11 Nylon nuts and bolts

Scales of production

REVISED

There are four main scales of production

- Prototype – this is an early example of a product that is produced as a 'one off' to test the concept or the process. A prototype can also be a bespoke product made for a particular purpose. An example of a prototype polymer-based product could an illuminated shop sign.
- Batch production – this involves producing a limited range of products. It usually involves the use of machinery. An example of polymer-based batch production could include the production of window frames.
- Mass production – this is where large quantities of identical products are made, and will almost certainly involve machinery. An example of polymer-based mass production could include the manufacture of lunch boxes.
- Continuous production – this involves the constant manufacture of products and would normally be carried out using fully-automated machinery. An example of polymer-based continuous production could include the manufacture of water bottles.

Specialist techniques and processes

REVISED

The use of production aids

Most production aids that are used with timber and metal-based materials are relevant to the use of polymers.

Tools, equipment and processes

There are a range of specific marking-out, cutting, shaping and joining methods used with polymer-based materials and it is important to know which ones to use.

Marking out

- A spirit-based pen will draw onto a polymer surface without scratching it.
- Paper templates will give extra protection to the shiny surface of the polymer.
- Keep the protective sheet on your polymer for as long as possible: it will help keep the surface clean and free from scratches.
- A laser cutter can be used to etch marking-out lines onto the surface of most polymers.

Sawing

- Most metal and woodworking saws will cut polymers. The coping saw will allow you to cut around curves in acrylic (PMMA).
- Laser cutters will produce very accurate, clean cuts in most polymers.
- A craft knife will cut thin polymer sheets such as the high impact polystyrene (HIPS) sheets used for vacuum forming.

Shaping

- Polymers can be filed and sanded into shape by traditional methods using metalworking files and abrasive papers such as 'wet or dry' paper.
- Thermoforming polymers can be shaped using a strip heater to produce a bend along a straight line.

- An oven can be used to soften a thermoforming polymer before it is shaped in a mould.
- Most cutting and shaping tools used in the manufacture of metal products can be used when making polymer-based components.

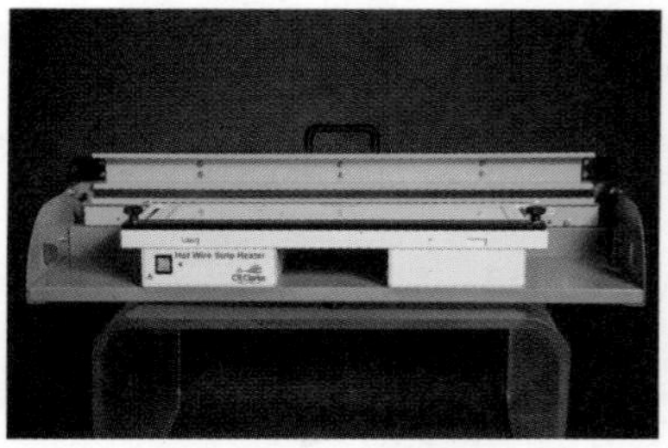

Forming polymers

There are a number of ways that polymers can be formed in the school workshop.

Figure 9.12 A strip heater

Line bending

Line bending using a strip heater is an effective way of producing a straight-line bend in acrylic (PMMA).

The line bending process:
- Place the acrylic sheet directly above the hot wire.
- Regularly check to see if the acrylic has softened as it heats up.
- Once softened, remove the sheet and bend to the desired angle. (A jig can help get the correct angle.)

Vacuum forming

The **vacuum-forming** machine will produce a three-dimensional polymer shape from a given mould.

Figure 9.13 A vacuum-formed product made from high impact polystyrene (HIPS)

The vacuum-forming process:
- Place the mould onto the platen.
- Lower the platen.
- Clamp the HIPS sheet onto the machine.
- Heat the HIPS until soft.
- Blow a dome (only necessary for tall moulds).
- Raise the platen.
- Switch on the vacuum.
- Remove the heat and allow to cool.
- Remove the mould from the HIPS and trim.

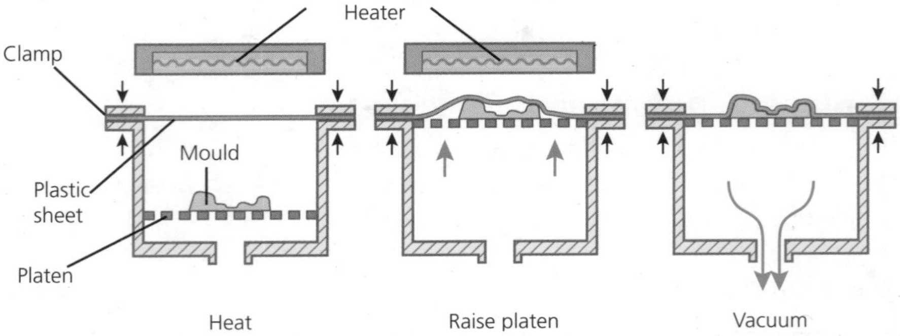

Heater

Clamp

Mould

Plastic sheet

Platen

Heat   Raise platen   Vacuum

Figure 9.14 The vacuum-forming process

Press forming

Thicker three-dimensional shapes can be produced by **press forming**.

The press-forming process:
- An acrylic (PMMA) sheet is warmed in an oven until soft.
- The sheet is placed over the 'plug'.
- The 'yoke' is placed over the top of the acrylic and pressure is applied.
- The acrylic sheet will take the shape of the mould.
- The acrylic sheet is then left to cool, removed from the mould and trimmed.

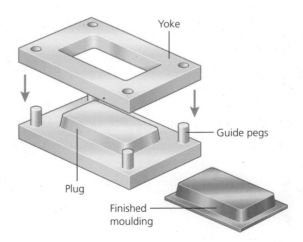

Yoke

Guide pegs

Plug

Finished moulding

Figure 9.15 A press-forming mould

Exam practice answers at **www.hoddereducation.co.uk/6 myrevisionnotesdownloads**

Commercial processes

Polymers lend themselves perfectly to commercial manufacturing processes.

● Most of these processes involve using expensive machinery and the production of high-quality moulds.

● This leads to high initial set-up costs and is only affordable when high volumes of a product are required.

Injection moulding

Many products that we use today are produced by **injection moulding**:

● For example: a chair, pen, smartphone case.

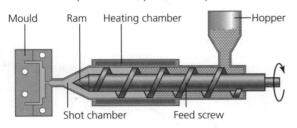

Figure 9.16 An injection-moulding machine

The injection-moulding process:

● Polymer granules are fed into the hopper which feeds the granules into the heating chamber.

● An Archimedean screw transports the granules along the heating chamber which gradually turns them into a molten state.

● The molten plastic is then injected into the pre-prepared mould.

● The mould is then cooled and the component is removed.

Extrusion

The process of **extruding** polymers produces a continuous section of product.

● For example: house guttering and rainwater piping.

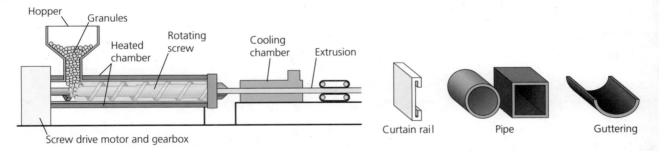

Figure 9.17 The extrusion process

The extrusion process:

● Polymer granules are fed into the hopper which feeds the granules into the heating chamber.

● An Archimedean screw transports the granules along the heating chamber which gradually turns them into a molten state.

● The molten polymer is then fed through a die that is the same cross-sectional shape as the finished product.

● The extruded polymer is gently pulled through the die to keep it in a uniform shape and gradually cooled.

● The extruded polymer can then be cut to length or coiled onto a roll.

> **Typical mistake**
>
> When asked to describe a commercial process used in the manufacture of polymer-based products, candidates will often produce weak, inaccurate diagrams.
>
> Make sure that you can draw an accurate, fully-labelled diagram of an industrial process such as injection moulding.

The application and use of quality control to include measurable and quantitative systems used during manufacture

Most of the details of cutting, shaping and forming to a tolerance have already been covered within the timber and metal-based material sections. However, there are some polymer-specific methods we should know about.

- Three-millimetre acrylic is the most popular thickness used when laser cutting.
- However, there are slight variations in this thickness that will have an effect on the performance of the laser.
- The thickness should be checked with a micrometre or vernier caliper and the power settings of the laser cutter altered.

Surface treatment and finishes

REVISED

Polymers are self-coloured, have an excellent surface finish and are naturally water-, chemical- and weather-resistant. Therefore, there is often no need to apply surface finishes.

Polishing

- Edges of a polymer may need finishing if they have been cut.
- This will usually involve filing the edge and then smoothing with abrasive papers.
- Finally, a polished surface can be achieved by polishing with a buffing machine and a liquid polishing compound.

Vacuum forming: a process that involves heating a thermoforming polymer and sucking it around a mould.

Press forming: the process of softening a thermoforming polymer and pressing it into a mould.

Injection moulding: an industrial process where polymer granules are heated and injected into a mould.

Extrusion: an industrial process involving heating polymer granules and forcing them through a die to produce long, uniform, cross-sectional polymer products.

Exam tip

Remember the names of every type of polymer: you should be able to describe their properties and give specific uses.

Now test yourself

TESTED

1 Name the main source of polymers. [1 mark]
2 Use notes and sketches to describe the process of fractional distillation. [4 marks]
3 Name the two categories of polymers. [2 marks]
4 Explain why polyethylene terephthalate (PET) is used in the manufacture of drinks bottles. [2 marks]
5 Use notes and sketches to describe the process of injection moulding. [4 marks]

Exam practice answers at **www.hoddereducation.co.uk/6 myrevisionnotesdownloads**

Exam practice

1 Which of the following is not a type of strength?

a) Compression   c) Shear

b) Ductility   d) Tension   [1 mark]

2 Which of the following is a suitable saw for cutting a curve in wood?

a) Hacksaw   c) Coping saw

b) Panel saw   d) Tenon saw   [1 mark]

3 Which of the following is a marking-out tool for metal?

a) Mortise gauge   c) Marking knife

b) Scriber   d) Try square   [1 mark]

4 Which of the following methods would be used to produce a yoghurt pot?

a) Injection moulding   c) Vacuum forming

b) Blow moulding   d) Rotational moulding   [1 mark]

5 Explain what is meant by the term 'deforestation'.   [1 mark]

6 Give two examples of the consequences of deforestation.   [2 marks]

7 Describe the consequences of polymers finding their way into the oceans.   [2 marks]

8 Name the four methods of converting timber.   [4 marks]

9 Explain why newly-converted timber should be seasoned.   [3 marks]

10 Name the source material of iron.   [1 mark]

11 Describe the environmental issues related to mining and processing metal ores.   [4 marks]

12 Name the process used to convert crude oil into naphtha.   [1 mark]

13 State the advantages of machining rather than etching a PCB.   [2 marks]

14 State the advantages of using jigs when manufacturing products.   [4 marks]

ONLINE

10 Investigation, primary and secondary data

Research is an essential part of designing and manufacturing products for clients and users. It is collected and used throughout the process, providing essential data and knowledge, which helps to produce a successful end product.

Using primary and secondary data to understand client and/or user needs

REVISED

- Research allows you to learn more about a subject and make decisions which help the user of the end product.
- Gathering data when you research will help you understand the needs of the client.
- **Primary research** – this means collecting the research information first-hand, for yourself. This can be in the form of questionnaires, interviews, observations and tests.
- **Secondary research** – this means using the research that somebody else has already collected (such as through books, magazines and the internet).

Market research

- This is carried out by manufacturers in order to gain an understanding of the person or people that they think will use their products.
- It can provide an accurate picture of the potential buyer for your product.
- Interviews and questionnaires are usually carried out at a face-to-face meeting.
- Questions are used to find out what people are thinking – this could be an expert or a group of people.
- The types of questions asked can be open or closed questions.
  - Open questions allow the interviewee more freedom in their answer to a question.
  - A closed question is more likely to only be answered with a short 'yes' or 'no' type response.
- Closed-question responses are easier to analyse.
- Designers need to consider **human factors** (issues relating to people), when they begin to design a product.
- Human factors can be categorised as:
  - physiological – the way in which people move and their physical attributes
  - psychological – the way a person reacts to new experiences
  - sociological – the effects a product will have on people.
- The way in which a user interacts with their environment is called **ergonomics**.

Focus groups

- **Focus groups** are also used to collect research, especially by big companies.
- This is a form of primary research and is a useful way of collecting the views of a large group of people.

> **Exam tip**
>
> Be able to analyse data collected as research in the form of graphs, charts and tables.

Exam practice answers at www.hoddereducation.co.uk/6 myrevisionnotesdownloads

Anthropometric data and percentiles

- A further example of primary research collected by a designer is **anthropometric** data.
- Measurements are taken from the human body and used to ensure the product fits the intended user or group.
- Graphs like the one below are used to show anthropometric data.
- The designer selects only relevant data which will help them to produce a product to suit the intended target audience.
- Usually those below the 5th percentile and above the 95th percentile are ignored, as these measurements are below and above average.

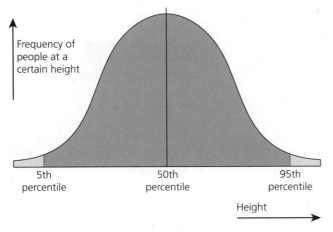

Figure 10.1 A percentile graph showing heights

Primary research: investigations carried out first hand.

Secondary research: using the investigations of others.

Human factors: issues relating to people.

Ergonomics: human interaction with products.

Focus group: a large group of people who feed back their opinions.

Anthropometrics: human dimensions.

How to write a design brief

REVISED

- A design brief is a statement outlining what is to be designed and made.
- It can be written most simply as 'Design and make …'
- Further details can be added to the brief to include a context and any details that research may have identified already.
- The design brief shows a clear understanding of the task and how problems will be solved.
- When you are given a design brief, you will need to analyse it by posing relevant questions which can then guide further research.

How to produce a design and manufacturing specification

- The design specification sets out the design constraints based on research that has been carried out.
- It is usually written as a list of clear statements relating to what the design must be, must do and must have.
- The design specification is referred to when designing and evaluating design ideas.
- A manufacturing specification contains all of the information needed to make the product and is produced after the final design idea has been developed.
- A manufacturing specification allows a third party to manufacture the product as it contains details about:
  - materials
  - components
  - tools
  - health and safety
  - sequence of making
  - **tolerances**.

Tolerance: the allowable amount of variation of a specified dimension within which quality can still be assured.

> **Typical mistake**
>
> Don't confuse a design specification with a manufacturing specification or confuse how they are used in the design process. Make sure that you know the difference.

Carrying out investigations in order to identify problems and needs

- The design brief may be altered by the designer throughout the process, in light of new problems or information being discovered.
- If further research and testing finds aspects that are critical to the success of the project and without which the project would not work, changes to the design brief should be made.

Now test yourself

1 Give three examples of primary research. [3 marks]
2 Explain the difference between ergonomics and anthropometrics. [2 marks]
3 What information is given in a manufacturing specification to allow a third party to manufacture the product? [3 marks]
4 Name the three categories of human factors considered by a designer. [3 marks]
5 Why might a design brief change throughout the process? [2 marks]

11 Environmental, social and economic challenge

Designing and making products has an impact on the environment. Understanding how to manage that impact is important.

Deforestation

- Trees are cut down to make timber/paper-based products and for grazing space for animals.
- Designers and manufacturers have a responsibility to source materials from **sustainably-**managed forests.
- Forest Stewardship Council® (FSC®)-certified products are made with materials from well-managed forests and/or verified and recycled sources.
- To reduce the impact their products have, designers and companies could:
  - use the most appropriate, responsibly sourced species for the application
  - use FSC-certified materials
  - introduce a zero-deforestation policy
  - set targets to maximise the use of recycled wood, pulp and paper.

Figure 11.1 FSC logo

Carbon dioxide levels and global warming

- Global warming is the increase in the average temperature of the Earth's atmosphere and oceans, which has been rising over recent years.
- Global warming occurs when carbon dioxide (CO_2) collects in the atmosphere.
- The gases absorb the sunlight reflecting off the Earth's surface and trap heat which is unable to escape. As a result the Earth gets hotter.
- Increased levels of CO_2 and other gases are a result of humans burning **fossil fuels**, vehicles in transport, land clearing and agriculture.
- Global warming is affecting weather patterns and sea levels as the polar ice caps are melting.
- Designers should try to reduce the impact their products have on the environment.

> **Exam tip**
>
> You may be asked to give examples of, either a product that has a negative effect on the environment, or a product that has been redesigned to lessen its impact. Make sure you know of examples that you can discuss at length.

Fair trade

- Fair trade is a trading partnership that works towards fair prices and better working conditions for farmers and workers who produce goods all around the world.
- People gain a fair price for their goods and are protected from **exploitation**.
- Fair trade supports developing communities, helping to protect the environment in which they live and work.
- The fair trade logo found on products shows that ingredients and materials have met fair trade standards.

Figure 11.2 Fair trade logo

Sustainability: design which considers the environmental impact, both in the long and short term.

Fossil fuels: finite resources such as coal, oil and gas.

Exploitation: the action or fact of treating someone unfairly in order to benefit from their work.

> **Typical mistake**
>
> This topic lends itself to discussion in the exam so try to be able to give the pros and cons of an argument and have products and examples to back up your discussion. If you give only basic facts and your argument lacks substance in a discussion-type question, you will not achieve the higher marks.

Now test yourself

1 Explain how global warming is changing the Earth.   [4 marks]
2 Give examples of products that would carry the fair trade logo.   [2 marks]
3 Explain the importance of using FSC materials in a new product.   [3 marks]
4 How does fair trade support workers?   [3 marks]
5 Discuss the role a designer plays in minimising the impact on the environment.   [6 marks]

Exam practice answers at **www.hoddereducation.co.uk/6 myrevisionnotesdownloads**

12 The work of others

Designers and design movements of the past have been influential in the design of the products we use today. They have changed the way we view products and continue to be a source of inspiration.

Designers

Harry Beck

- In 1931 Harry Beck created the London Underground map, showing the ever-expanding network in the simplest way.
- Beck's solution was based on an electrical wiring diagram using angular and diagonal lines.
- This simple design is now used for transport maps all around the world.

Marcel Breuer

- Marcel Breuer was a student and teacher at the Bauhaus school in Germany from 1920 to 1928.
- Breuer used new materials and technologies, especially tubular steel because of its affordability and the fact it could easily be used in mass manufacture, to produce furniture.
- His **iconic** products, such as the Wassily chair, were seen to be beautiful but functional and **geometric**. The Wassily chair is still copied and sold today.

Figure 12.1 The Wassily chair

Iconic: product which is held in high regard, is well known, has influenced others and withstood the test of time.

Geometric: use of shapes and angles in design.

Contemporary: present-day design.

Innovative: advanced or original.

Norman Foster

- Norman Foster is a British architect who partnered Richard Rogers to build housing in the UK.
- Forster's architecture is a high-tech, **contemporary** style, which considers environmental impact and involves the **innovative** use of materials and technology.
- He is known for creating large open spaces within buildings and uses materials such as steel and glass to achieve this.

Sir Alec Issigonis

- After studying engineering, Alec Issigonis joined Morris Motors in 1936 as a suspension designer.
- There, he developed the Morris Minor, which remained in production from 1948 to 1971.
- Issigonis then went on to develop the Mini in 1959. This was a reliable car which was particularly small and compact, yet had enough space for four passengers.
- The Mini was revolutionary as it had a transverse engine (turned 190°), which is what allowed it to be more compact.

Figure 12.2 The Mini

William Morris

- William Morris was founder of the Arts and Crafts movement in the nineteenth century and set up his own business in 1861.
- Morris is best known for his highly decorative wallpaper and furnishings, using nature and natural forms to inspire his patterns.
- His furniture designs were hand crafted and **ornate**.
- Morris famously said about design: 'Have nothing in your house that you do not know to be useful, or believe to be beautiful.'

> **Ornate**: highly decorative.

Louis Comfort Tiffany

- Louis Tiffany was an American designer famous for his glassware in the nineteenth century.
- By 1890 he was a leading glass producer, experimenting with ways of colouring the material.
- As well as decorating part of the White House in Washington, Tiffany is most famous for his stained-glass lamps.
- His designs were based around nature.

Raymond Templier

- Raymond Templier was a French jewellery designer born in 1891.
- He worked in the family jewellery business but designed **cubist**-style pieces which used geometric patterns.
- Templier's work used mainly lacquer and enamels, along with white gold and silver.
- He was also known for using dark stones such as onyx to contrast with the metals.

Figure 12.3 'Dragonfly' Tiffany lamp

Gerrit Reitveld

- Gerrit Reitveld designed for mass production. His designs were simple and suitable for machine production.
- He was heavily influenced by the De Stijl movement and designed the Red and Blue chair in 1917.
- Reitveld transformed the traditional bulky arm chair into a work of art.
- From 1928 he focused on architecture, designing in a more **functional** way.
- He designed social housing using prefabricated concrete slabs. His aim was to create more affordable housing. To achieve this, he used **standardised** materials and assembly lines to lower costs.

> **Cubist**: early twentieth-century design, making use of geometry and interlocking planes.
>
> **Functional**: an object which works well and fulfils its purpose or job.
>
> **Standardised**: all parts are the same and identical so can be replaced easily.

Figure 12.4 The iconic Red and Blue chair

Charles Rennie Macintosh

- Charles Rennie Macintosh was a Scottish designer who was linked to the Art Nouveau movement.

Exam practice answers at **www.hoddereducation.co.uk/6 myrevisionnotesdownloads**

- Macintosh attended the Glasgow School of Art along with the Macdonald sisters and Herbert Macnair – they became known as 'The Four'.
- Macintosh is best known for his [iconic] chairs, [chair designs] and for the design of the Glasgow School of Art.

Aldo Rossi

- Also Rossi was an Italian architect and product designer.
- He wanted his buildings to respect their environment and blend into the architecture of the area.
- His first building, the cemetery in San Cataldo, Modena, used geometry and symmetry to mirror the local factories of the area.

Figure 12.5 Cemetery in San Cataldo

- Rossi was also connected to the Italian design group Alessi and was known for his sleek coffee makers which used stainless steel.

Ettore Sottsass

- Ettore Sottsass was an influential Italian designer who was part of the Memphis design movement.
- He designed a wide and varied range of products, from furniture to jewellery.
- Sottsass later worked for the Italian design group Alessi.
- He wanted his products not only to fulfil a function but also to suggest a new way to function.

Philippe Starck

- Philippe Starck is a contemporary French designer who pushes the boundaries of design.
- He worked for the Alessi design group, producing **postmodernistic** designs.
- His most famous product is the Juicy Salif, a lemon squeezer which is more of a statement piece than a functional product.

> **Postmodernistic**: designs which consider the aesthetics of an object more than the functionality.

> **Exam tip**
>
> You only need to know about two of these designers for the exam. Choose two designers that you are interested in to revise.

> **Typical mistake**
>
> If you don't have a depth of knowledge about two designers and movements, you won't be able to discuss their work in detail. You should be able to make reference to the style of specific products they have designed, knowing enough to be able to form arguments. Superficial facts will not allow you to do this.

Companies

Alessi

- Alessi is a family-run design company founded in 1921 by Giovanni Alessi.
- The company is known for producing designer products, from chairs to kitchenware.
- Many iconic designers have worked with Alessi, including Richard Sapper, Ettore Sottsass and Philippe Starck.
- Alessi products place importance on personality and interest, creativity and the use of colour. Often made of metal, they are designed to be mass produced.
- The products are not always the most functional.

Apple

- Apple is famous for producing electronics and computer software.
- The company has produced the iPod, iPhone and Mac personal computer.
- Apple was founded by Steve Jobs, Steve Wozniak and Ronald Wayne in 1976. Also associated with Apple is Jonathan Ive.
- Ive is chief designer and has over 5,000 **patents.** He has won many design awards for his work.
- Apple products are sleek and stylish and the technology they use is fundamental to their successful design.

Braun

- Braun is a German design company, designing small appliances.
- In 1929 Max Braun began making radio components, later producing entire radios.
- His company became one of the biggest in Germany, branching out into other electrical items.
- Braun is known for its functionality and its use of colour during the **pop art** period.
- For 30 years, Dieter Rams was the head of design. Today his work is shown in the Museum of Modern Art in New York.

Dyson

- James Dyson invented the first bagless vacuum cleaner after producing 5,127 **prototypes.**
- The Dyson DC01 used 'cyclone technology' to increase suction.
- Other inventions by Dyson include the contra-rotating washing machine (having two drums inside) and the hand dryer.

> **Patent**: a form of intellectual property which protects a designer's ideas.
>
> **Pop art**: art based on modern popular culture.
>
> **Prototype:** a first or initial version of a product.

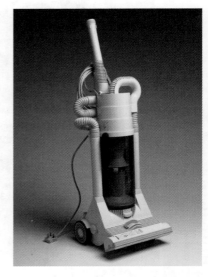

Figure 12.6 The first Dyson vacuum cleaner

> **Exam tip**
>
> You only need to know about two of these companies for the exam. Choose two companies that you are interested in to revise.

Now test yourself

1 For a designer of your choice, list ten facts. [5 marks]
2 Which designers have worked for the design company Alessi and what design are they most famous for producing? [2 marks]
3 Sketch and explain a product by a designer from the list above. [3 marks]
4 What do the terms postmodernism, pop art and cubism mean? [3 marks]
5 For a designer of your choice, discuss the reasons that their work is considered iconic. [4 marks]

Exam practice answers at **www.hoddereducation.co.uk/6 myrevisionnotesdownloads**

13 Design strategies

Design strategies give you ways of using imagination and creativity as you start the design process.

Generate imaginative and creative design ideas using a range of different design strategies

Not all successful designs come from professional product designers. Sometimes people see an opportunity and rise to the challenge.

Collaboration – working together

- Large companies such as Rolls Royce have design teams working together to solve problems. Tasks are analysed and solutions explored as a group, sharing ideas.
- Putting everyone's ideas together results in a wider range of resources to choose from as you begin the design process.
- Work that seems daunting to do on your own, such as the **task analysis**, can be easier to do as a group sharing questions and thoughts. For example, at the start of your project you could work collaboratively to analyse a set brief and then move on to answer the questions individually to progress with your project.
- Research for a project can also be carried out collaboratively (for example, visiting a local store to look at existing products). In a group, you can share thoughts and questions about the information you have found.
- Collaborative work can help you gain confidence as you work through your project.

User-centred design

- Problem solving – products are sometimes invented when a problem is discovered. For example, James Dyson's ballbarrow replaces the wheel with a ball to prevent it sinking into mud.
- Client-based approach – when using a client for your project, ensure that they are available to help and support you throughout the process. They should help you to agree the design specification and give feedback on ideas, as well as evaluations.
- Designing through customer feedback – this can help a product to **evolve** when alternative suggestions are put forward. Focus groups can be used to do this when testing a new product.
- Market research companies are available to assist design companies with their research. They use databanks of customers' needs which have been taken from their online searches.

> **Task analysis:** looking at the design task or brief in depth and asking questions.
>
> **Evolve:** to develop gradually.

A systems approach

- A system is a group of interconnected parts that does something. Dealing with these parts can be complex, so a 'systems approach' is used.
- What the system is trying to achieve is known as the 'systems goal'.
- 'Systems thinking' involves looking at the whole problem, not just the component parts.
- Systems can be divided into two types:
  - ○ hard systems that are machine- or hardware-dominated
  - ○ soft systems where the actions of humans decide what happens.
- Hard systems are easier to model as they have set behaviours (for example, a switch is either on or off).
- An example of a system is a car. This has lots of interconnected parts but without a driver or fuel it won't work. When there are lots of cars, rules need to be put in place.
- Complex systems can be divided into sub-systems (for example, in a car there is the braking system and steering system).
- Block diagrams can be used to show how a system works.
- Most systems rely on feedback, either negative (keeps a constant) or positive (magnifies something).
- A flow chart is used to show what happens in a system. It uses standard symbols.

Iterative design

- This means using prototypes, testing and analysis to refine a product.
- In your project, client feedback will help to refine design ideas further.
- Modelling will allow you to test out your ideas and help to solve problems, leading to further design development.

Avoiding design fixation

- Use a wide range of sources to help you find inspiration as you start your designs.
- Geometric pattern is a good starting point and has been used by many famous designers (such as Mary Quant and Marc Jacobs).
- Geometry is used in both surface patterns and 3D design (for example, the Braun geometrical kettle by Emi Schenkelbach).
- Mathematical patterns are also a starting point. Fibonacci introduced his sequence in 1202. In the Fibonacci sequence, every number after the first two is the sum of the two preceding ones: 0, 1, 1, 2, 3, 5, 8, 13, 21, 34, 55, 89, 144.
- Designing from natural forms – **biomimicry** is an approach which looks to nature for inspiration. Nature has already solved many of the problems that we encounter.
- Shape and pattern in nature can be seen in the work of many famous designers, for example Cath Kidston.

> **Biomimicry:** the design of products modelled on nature.

Golden Ratio

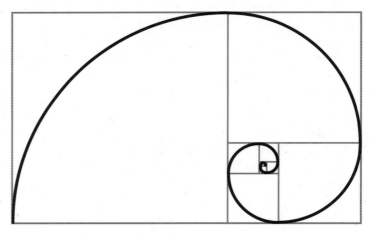

Figure 13.1 Fibonacci squares

- Natural images can be used to help with your designs but it is useful to adapt the pattern and shape of natural forms.
- Cultural influences – the Great Exhibition took place in London in 1851. It was the first exhibition to celebrate cultural and industrial product design.
- It is now easier to travel and connect through social media and the internet, so we can easily see designs from around the world.

Explore and develop your own ideas

REVISED

The following design strategies should provide a starting point in designing and developing ideas. You should also consider how social and environmental factors influence design.

Sketching

- Use the best tools available.
- Show different aspects of the design.
- Keep sketches clear and accurate.
- Keep notes simple and precise.
- Spend time designing which aspects of the idea could be improved.
- 3D drawings can help to communicate clearly.

Modelling

- This helps test out ideas quickly and can be done in foam, card, fabric or wire.
- It tests **proportions** and sizes.
- A full-size mock-up in cheaper material can be useful to show construction techniques.
- CAD/CAM makes it quicker to make and change models.
- A full-size mock-up in textiles is called a toile.
- Construction kits can be used to model mechanical systems.
- Electronic systems can be modelled using virtual circuits where component values can be changed and the effect on the circuit tested.

> **Proportion**: sizes in relation to one another.

Testing

- Testing should be carried out as you design and manufacture your product.
- Comparison tables and client feedback will help you decide which ideas to develop further.
- You can test the ergonomics of a product to make sure it suits the user.
- Materials and construction methods can also be tested to ensure success.
- In systems, circuits can be tested on prototype boards, known as 'breadboarding', using real components.
- Surface finishes can also be sampled and tested for suitability.

Evaluation of work to improve outcomes

- Along with testing, you will need to:
  - evaluate results
  - carry out improvements
  - refine your design.
- Your design specification can be used as a checklist to help you evaluate and should continue to be used as your project progresses.
- It is useful in your **summative** evaluation to compare your prototype to other similar products on the market.
- Be critical as you evaluate – this will help your product to improve as you develop it.
- Ask your client to test and evaluate your end product.

> **Summative**: assessing the whole process after completion.

Now test yourself

TESTED

1. Describe three ways in which designers find inspiration to produce their design ideas. [3 marks]
2. Discuss the benefits of using the client throughout the design and manufacture process. [4 marks]
3. Explain how using a collaborative approach to design can be beneficial. [2 marks]

Exam practice answers at **www.hoddereducation.co.uk/6 myrevisionnotesdownloads**

14 Communication of design ideas

There are many different techniques that can be used to communicate ideas and the designer's intent clearly to the client.

Freehand sketching

REVISED

- Freehand sketching is done without the use of drawing aids.
- Ideas can be expressed quickly this way.
- Knowing the basics and practising them will build confidence.
- Using a mechanical pencil will allow for consistent line quality.
- Start with 2D freehand sketching to gain confidence. A starting point could be to take the five shapes shown and sketch them as 2D shapes.

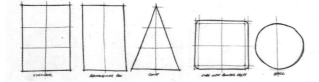

Figure 14.1 Freehand two-dimensional sketches of three-dimensional forms

- Sketches can be enhanced by adding thick and thin lines and colour **rendering** techniques.

Figure 14.2 Enhanced sketches

- Lightly sketching out the framework of a shape is a good starting point. This is called **crating** and the lines can then be added in bold.
- Adding a faint centre line to a drawing can add detail and also help with rendering.
- There is no set rule when it comes to adding darker or more weighted lines, but it is effective when added to **concave** curved edges.

> **Rendering**: adding colour to a drawing to enhance communication.
>
> **Crating**: a series of faint lines which help to build the final sketch.
>
> **Concave**: a surface that curves inwards.
>
> **Tone**: the deepness or brightness of a shade of colour.

Thick and thin lines

- The outline is a continuous and connected line that defines the outer boundary of an object. It is the boldest and thickest line of all.
- Use either a fine liner or outline pen to add this darker, thicker line to the outside edges of the design.

Rendering techniques

- Add colour, or texture, to enhance a sketch to better communicate design intent.
- Coloured pencils can be used to effectively add **tone** when rendering.
- Marker pens with layout paper also work well and allow a flat colour wash to be achieved.
- To sketch freehand in 3D, take a 2D idea or drawing and translate this into 3D.

2D and 3D drawings

REVISED

Isometric

- Isometric means 'equal measure'.
- 30° angles are applied to the sides of an object to give a 3D effect.
- This gives a more constructed way of showing an idea.
- Isometric grid paper makes it easier to draw in this style.
- Objects don't look realistic as there is no **perspective** applied to the drawing.

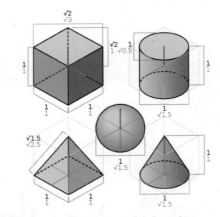

Figure 14.3 Isometric drawing

Perspective drawing

- Objects look more realistic as drawings tend to get smaller when they get closer to the vanishing lines drawn as a guide on the horizon line.
- One-point perspective drawing shows how things appear to get smaller as they get further away, **converging** towards a single 'vanishing point' on the horizon line.
- This is a popular drawing method for illustrators and architects to show objects from the front view or to look down something long, such as into a room.
- Two-point perspective drawing is a more realistic way to show 3D objects.
- Two vanishing points are used on the horizon line, one at either end.
- A vertical line is used to show the front corner of the object being drawn and other lines go to the vanishing points.
- Shadows: adding a shadow can make your 3D sketch look more realistic, as though your object is sitting on a surface, giving it weight.
- Linking boxes: these can be added to a design page to connect similar ideas together.
- Organic form: non-geometric shapes are more difficult to draw in 3D.
- Try to sketch out the idea in 2D form first showing different viewpoints.

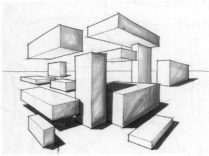

Figure 14.4 Two-point perspective drawing

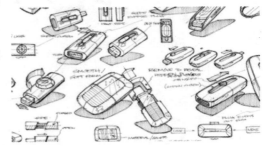

Figure 14.5 Sketch demonstrating use of shadows

Exam practice answers at **www.hoddereducation.co.uk/6 myrevisionnotesdownloads**

Design ideas and sketches – a good way to start

- Designers use inspiration boards to generate ideas.
- Look at nature, mathematical patterns, existing products, your user's likes, architecture, the work of others and technological developments, to gain inspiration.
- From this, take shapes, colour, patterns and forms that inspire you. Make a cardboard window to focus into a part of an image and make it into a pattern.
- Images can be scanned into a software program to be **manipulated** further.
- Start the design section of your work with a sheet of thumbnail sketches to show a range of ideas.
- You don't need to filter out ideas that you don't like at this stage.
- Rendering isn't essential on thumbnail sketches but you could use a fine liner to highlight aspects of designs.
- 2D drawings are useful for this process as they are quicker to draw and put your thinking onto paper.
- Show evidence of how your research has influenced your designing.
- Refine ideas by considering materials and manufacture – begin to research these areas.
- Use all of your research findings to begin to develop ideas to a point where you can choose one or two to take further and develop.

Figure 14.6 Thumbnail sketches

> **Perspective**: the height, width and depth of an object drawn in relation to each other.
>
> **Converging**: meeting at a point.
>
> **Manipulated**: changed and controlled to fit the design.
>
> **Annotation**: text and comments added to a diagram to give explanation.

System and schematic diagrams

- These allow you to think logically about a problem and how to solve it.
- A good systems diagram shows where every process can be divided into input, process and output:
  - Input: the problems and questions you are trying to solve.
  - Process: the electrical and mechanical elements included in your design
  - Output: what you think will be the end product.
- A schematic diagram uses symbols rather than realistic images. In fashion design, these diagrams are called 'flats' as no body is drawn.

Annotated drawings

- Remember to describe, explain and discuss your ideas in order to communicate them clearly.
- **Annotation** can help to clarify your design intention as sketches may not be able to show all of your ideas on paper.
- Describe: the shape and form of the design and whether it has any resemblance to other products, objects or architecture.
- Explain: giving explanations of materials, construction, scale and size, functionality and features.
- Discuss: what else do you need to state that the design drawing can't show? Can you give reasons for your decisions?

Exploded diagrams

- These are drawings which show the parts of a product separated out.
- Details such as construction, joining methods, strengthening methods or internal fittings can be shown.
- You can produce this type of drawing by tracing your 3D sketch, one part at a time, moving the original drawing so that the parts are not connected together.

Working drawings

- A **scale drawing** of your chosen idea can be used to construct and manufacture your idea.
- This can be drawn out by hand or using software packages. The drawing must be precise.
- They usually consist of a front, side and plan (top) view of the product.
- First- and third-angle orthographic drawings are the most common working drawings used.
- Dimensions are added to allow for manufacture (these are written above arrow lines, showing the measurements).

> **Scale drawing**: a drawing with accurate sizes that have been enlarged or reduced by a certain amount.

Audio and visual recordings

These can be added into your work to support your designing in the following ways:

- Interview a client for feedback.
- Explore a client's needs and problems first hand.
- You could explain your ideas more clearly verbally.
- Video a test model to look at comfort and ergonomics.
- Analyse and disassemble a product, explaining your findings.

Computer-based tools

- CAD can be used alongside a laser cutter to produce card models quickly and accurately.
- Virtual modelling: software allows for photorealistic 3D models to be produced and rendered.
- CAD helps to visualise the product when it is made. It can:
  - check sizes and proportions
  - test out different colour schemes and materials
  - place the product into context or a scene.

Figure 14.7 Exploded diagram

Modelling

- This allows you to appreciate your idea in 3D and can be tested out by your client.
- Details of the functionality and construction can be understood more clearly and problems solved.
- An idea or elements of different ideas that best solve the problem are modelled into a 3D form so that all views are understood.
- Modelling using card, styrofoam, MDF and modelling board are preferable as they are low cost and can be worked with quickly.
- Photographs of modelling and testing can be used to help with further development work.
- Evidence of development is crucial for your project as it demonstrates your ability to refine, evaluate and test an idea, along with continuing to research to solve problems.
- A product develops and becomes more accurate until it becomes a 'product prototype'. This allows for testing of manufacture, time, processes and assembly, which reduces mistakes and lowers costs in the long run.
- Foam modelling: styrofoam (blue and green foam) allows for 3D models to be made using hand tools, and finished using 'wet and dry' paper to give an accurate representation of the product.
- Foam-core board is lightweight and used for architectural models.
- Card modelling: corrugated card is normally used as it is available in different thicknesses and can be cut and joined easily.

Figure 14.8 Styrofoam model

> **Exam tip**
>
> Be able to identify the types of drawings highlighted in this chapter as you may be asked to redraw, complete or translate them in the exam.

> **Typical mistake**
>
> When asked to annotate in the exam, giving brief descriptions rather than explanations will cause you to miss out on the higher marks.

Now test yourself

1 What views are shown in an orthographic drawing? [3 marks]
2 Why are perspective drawings more useful than isometric? [1 mark]
3 List five common modelling materials and reasons they are useful. [5 marks]
4 Describe how CAD can be used to produce a prototype. [2 marks]

15 Prototype development

Producing prototypes or models is an essential part of the designing and making process. It allows testing to be carried out and client feedback to be collected to help refine a product further.

Designing and developing prototypes

- First models are basic to test out a concept.
- Client feedback is used to refine an idea and produce further models.
- Prototypes are usually made from cheaper materials although systems may be modelled with real components to allow for testing.
- Common materials used in modelling include: paper, card, MDF, polystyrene, foam board, plastics, clay, calico and breadboards.

Satisfying the requirements of the brief

- The client sets the design brief, which includes the required features.
- Prototyping helps the designer work out how to meet the brief.
- Small sections of the product can be modelled to check construction.

Responding to client wants and needs

- Commercial manufacture makes use of CAD and CAM to prototype ideas.
- To avoid expense and save time, CAD is used to develop products virtually to allow designers to see the design working.
- Clients can also test the product using these **virtual models** and suggest improvements.
- Prototypes are part of the manufacturing specification to show the manufacturer how the product will look and function.

Demonstrating innovation

- Physical prototypes can be used to see if the design appeals to the target market and is suitable for manufacture on a large scale.
- This tends to be for innovative products that are ahead of their time.
- Sometimes these innovations remain as prototypes and do not go into large-scale production.

Functionality

- Testing a product's performance is important to ensure that materials, money and time are used efficiently.
- Size and ergonomics can be tested using full-scale prototypes.
- In fashion, prototypes are used to check how the garment fits and drapes when worn.

> **Typical mistake**
>
> When asked in the exam to explain the benefits of using CAD and CAM to produce prototypes, you will miss out on marks if you give only superficial answers (such as they are 'quick').

Figure 15.1 Concept car used to test market appeal

> **Virtual model:** a model produced using CAD software to understand the product without actually making it.

Exam practice answers at **www.hoddereducation.co.uk/6 myrevisionnotesdownloads**

Aesthetics

- Fashion and trends often determine the colours, shapes and patterns used.
- CAD allows designers to experiment with these elements quickly and easily.
- Fashion designers make use of this to show different colours and fabrics on a design.

Marketability

- Rapid prototyping allows a small number of products to be made economically.
- Rapid prototyping uses CNC machines to model quickly and in 3D.
- Complex shapes can be produced in this way.
- Prototypes made in this way can demonstrate how the product will look and function. The designer/manufacturer can understand how marketable the product will be.
- Feedback received can be used to improve the product and reactions from the target audience can be judged.

Figure 15.2 A cube being produced using a 3D printer

Evaluating prototypes

- A designer will test a prototype to ensure that the product is fit for its intended purpose.
- When you test your own models, it is important to get genuine client feedback.
- As a result of this feedback, modifications can be made and more models generated, to ensure that the end product is as suitable as it can be.
- In commercial manufacture, testing involves the client, members of the target market, experts in design and manufacture and experts in the use of the type of product.
- Focus groups are also used to gain the opinion of potential users.
- Prototypes are tested to ensure:
  - functionality
  - fitness for purpose
  - safety in use and manufacture
  - efficiency of manufacture.
- Final prototypes will be used to work out costings for materials and labour.

> **Exam tips**
>
> Be able to discuss the use of prototypes in both commercial (mass) production and one-off production.
>
> Be able to discuss specific examples of where prototypes have clearly been used effectively to develop a product further.

Now test yourself

TESTED

1 Describe how commercial manufacture makes use of CAD and CAM. [6 marks]
2 Explain the benefits of prototyping using 3D printers. [3 marks]
3 Explain why evaluating prototypes is an important part of the design and make process. [4 marks]
4 Why are prototypes tested? [3 marks]

16 Timber-based materials

In the exam you will only need to answer questions on this content in relation to one material category or system. You only need to revise this topic if you plan to answer questions with a focus on timber-based materials.

Selection of materials and components

There are many different types of wood and each has its own particular properties. When designing and making wooden prototypes it is essential to be able to select the most suitable timber.

Functional need

- Oak is a very strong, durable and attractive timber, which makes it suited to high-quality furniture.
- Teak is naturally weather-resistant, making it a good material for garden furniture.
- Balsa is a lightweight timber that is very easy to shape. This makes it ideally suited for model making.

Cost

Financial cost

The cost of wood varies considerably and a designer must take this into consideration if selling a wooden product for profit.

Figure 16.1 A softwood roof truss

- Rough sawn softwoods are relatively inexpensive and are extensively used in the construction of houses.
- Exotic woods such as rosewood are expensive and can only be used on high-quality, expensive, luxury wooden products.
- Manufactured boards are cost-effective and are used in the manufacture of affordable flat-pack furniture.

Environmental cost

- Natural timber is a renewable resource and has less impact on the environment than either metal- or polymer-based products.
- Manufactured boards have a greater environmental cost as they have undergone more processing and are not as easy to recycle.

Availability

Timber-based materials are readily available and very easy to obtain.

- Natural wood is sold as either rough sawn, planes square edge (PSE) or planed all round (PAR).
- It is available in standard sizes, which helps when costing a project.
- Manufactured boards are available in large sheets (2440 x 1220 mm) and in a variety of thicknesses.

Tolerances

It is difficult to design and manufacture using timber-based material to fine **tolerances** as natural timbers are not dimensionally stable.

- Natural timber will expand and contract, depending on how much moisture is in the air.
- Natural timber can bow, twist and warp as it dries out.
- Manufactured boards are far more stable. This makes them far more suitable to being cut to finer tolerances using CNC machinery such as a 3D router.
- A tolerance is needed to ensure that a component will be manufactured to an acceptable, functional size.

Material management

Cutting efficiently and minimising waste

- Wherever possible, stock-sized timber should be used as this will minimise waste.
- The use of templates will help ensure that wooden products are cut correctly first time.
- Shapes should be tessellated to use material as efficiently as possible.
- Wooden waste can be recycled or turned into a fuel.

Using appropriate marking-out methods, data points and co-ordinates

Stock timber must be flat and square before marking out can begin.

- A plane is used to make timber flat and square before marking out.
- **Face side** and **face edge** marks are placed on timber to show the flat square surfaces.

Specialist marking-out tools can speed up the marking-out process and increase accuracy and consistency.

- A try square will produce an accurate 90° line to an edge and is used as a datum reference.
- A marking gauge produces a straight line parallel to an edge.
- A mortise gauge produces a double straight line parallel to an edge.
- Time spent checking measurements for accuracy will reduce the chance of wasting both time and materials.

Specialist tools, equipment, techniques and processes

There are a number of specialist tools that can be used in the school workshop that will speed up the production of timber-based products and increase their accuracy and consistency.

- A 3D router can machine wood in three dimensions from a given CAD drawing.
- Laser cutters are commonly used with polymers but can also cut and engrave thin sections of timber.

> **Tolerance**: the acceptable difference between the upper and lower given sizes.
>
> **Face side and face edge**: two adjacent surfaces of wood that have been planed flat and square.

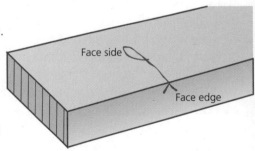

Figure 16.2 Face side and face edge marks

> **Typical mistake**
>
> Make sure that you don't confuse the names of marking-out equipment. For example, don't mix up a 'try square' with a 'set square'.

- A vacuum bag can be used when veneering or laminating wood.
- Steam bending enables solid sections of wood to be curved.
- Dovetail and dowelling jigs can be used to machine cut accurate joints.
- The correct PPE (personal protection equipments) equipment should be used at all times to ensure the safety of the user. For example, use ear defenders when using loud machinery; use a dust mask when sanding; and use leather gloves when handling hot or sharp metal.

Exam tip

Make sure that you know the correct names for specialist technical equipment.

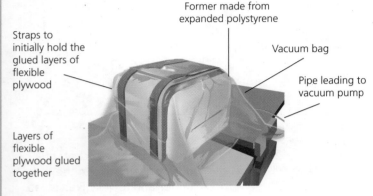

Former made from expanded polystyrene

Straps to initially hold the glued layers of flexible plywood

Vacuum bag

Pipe leading to vacuum pump

Layers of flexible plywood glued together

Figure 16.3 The vacuum bag

Surface treatments and finishes

Specialist surface finishes and treatments can be used to enhance the appearance (aesthetics) and to improve the weather resistance of timber-based products (function).

- The surface should be sanded smooth and cleaned so that it is free from dust, grease or oil.
- Wood stains, varnishes, oils and lacquers can be sprayed onto wooden products rather than applied with a brush. This is a much quicker process and produces a better-quality finish.
- **Tanilising** involves subjecting timber to high-pressure treatment using a wood preservative. This gives the material very good resistance to weathering and rot.
- Manufactured boards are often laminated with a thermosetting polymer such as melamine formaldehyde (MF) to give them a decorative surface that is waterproof, durable and heat proof. This process is extensively used to produce kitchen worktops.

Tanilising: a method of pressure treating wood with a preservative.

Now test yourself

TESTED

1 Name a suitable timber for garden furniture. [1 mark]
2 What is meant by the terms PSE and PAR? [2 marks]
3 Explain why it is difficult to work wood to very fine tolerances. [3 marks]
4 Use notes and sketches to show how you would use a vacuum bag to produce a laminated, curved piece of wood. [4 marks]
5 Name one method of changing the colour of wood. [1 mark]

Exam practice answers at **www.hoddereducation.co.uk/6 myrevisionnotesdownloads**

17 Metal-based materials

Selection of materials and components REVISED

One of the main reasons for selecting metal for use when manufacturing a prototype is because strength is a priority. However, metals do have many other properties that designers and manufacturers must be aware of.

Functional need

- Steel is strong and easy to join together. It is used extensively in the automotive industry.
- Aluminium is lightweight and has good resistance to corrosion. This makes it the ideal material for making aeroplanes.
- Copper has good electrical and thermal conductivity, which is why it can be found inside wiring.

Cost

Financial cost

- Low carbon steels are inexpensive.
- **Semi-precious** metals such as copper and tin are more expensive.
- **Precious** metals such a gold and silver are very expensive.

Environmental cost

- Sourcing and processing metals can have a negative effect on the environment.
- However, all metals can be recycled.

> **Semi-precious metal:** metal such as copper, that is more expensive than common metals such as steel.
>
> **Precious metal:** a rare metal that is expensive, such as gold.

Availability

- Metals are easy to get hold of and come in stock forms.

Tolerances REVISED

Metal components can be made to fine tolerances as most metals are hard and stable.

- Metal can be machined to a tolerance of 0.01 mm.
- Metals expand and contract with heat and sometimes this needs to be taken into consideration.
- The use of CNC machinery allows metal-based components to be produced to fine tolerances.
- Working to tolerance ensures that metal-based components will fit together and that the prototype will function as planned.

Material management

Cutting efficiently and minimising waste

It is important to design and make metal components using stock forms to minimise cutting and the production of waste.

- Casting processes redistribute metal and minimise waste.
- Machining processes such as turning, milling and drilling produce waste which, in industry, is recycled.
- Tessellating shapes can help to minimise waste.

Using appropriate marking-out methods, data points and co-ordinates

There is a wide range of specialist marking-out equipment that can be used on metal. Using metal-specific marking-out tools will help increase the accuracy and quality of the prototype.

- A surface plate gives a very smooth surface to mark out on.
- A scribing block helps produce accurate scribed lines.
- Angle plates will hold metal at an angle of 90° to the surface plate.
- A vee block will hold round bars when marking out.

Datum points and co-ordinates are essential when machining metal.

- A **datum** point is a known point.
- When using any **CNC** machines, such as a lathe, the tool will go to a 'home' position. This is a known position from where it will take all its measurements.
- *x*,*y* and *z* co-ordinates control the movement of a machine tool in one of three directions. This allows accurate components to be manufactured from a CAD drawing.

> **Datum point**: a known starting point.
>
> **CNC**: computer numerically controlled.

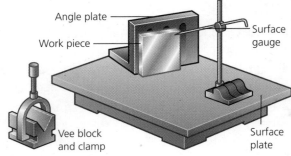

Figure 17.1 A surface plate with scribing block and vee blocks

> **Typical mistake**
>
> Make sure that you don't confuse wood- and metal-specific tools and equipment. For example, remember that an 'engineer's square' is different from a 'try square'.

Specialist tools, equipment, techniques and processes

There are a large number of specialist/industrial tools and equipment that can be used to manufacture metal components.

- A CNC lathe can parallel turn, face off, taper turn and even cut screw threads.
- A CNC milling machine can cut slots, grooves and machine edges and create flat, smooth surfaces in metal.
- Both machines follow CAD drawings to a high level of accuracy.
- They are faster and more consistent than machining by traditional methods on a centre lathe or a milling machine.
- A plasma cutter performs similar operations to a laser cutter but can cut and engrave quite large thicknesses of metal.
- The correct PPE equipment should be used at all times to ensure the safety of the user. For example, use goggles to prevent damage to your eyes caused by flying swarf.

Figure 17.2 A CNC lathe

Surface treatments and finishes

There are a number of specialist/industrial finishing processes used to increase the durability (functionality) and enhance the appearance (aesthetics) of metals.

- The surface should be free from dust, grease or oil. This can be achieved by cleaning with abrasive materials such as emery cloth and chemical cleaners such as white spirit.
- Steel can be galvanised to increase its resistance to corrosion.
- **Galvanising** involves dipping the steel into a bath of molten zinc.
- Car bodies are now galvanised before they are painted to increase the life of the car.
- The aluminium components of a mountain bike are anodised to help protect them from corrosion, harden the surface and improve their appearance.
- **Anodising** is an electrolytic process that involves passing a charge through an electrolytic bath that coats the aluminium in a protective, coloured oxide.

> **Galvanising**: a protective coating of zinc applied to the surface of steel.
>
> **Anodising**: a protective oxide layer applied to the surface of aluminium.

> **Exam tip**
>
> Make sure that you know an industrial method of finishing metal.

Figure 17.3 A plasma cutter

Now test yourself

1 Name a suitable metal used for knives, forks and spoons. [1 mark]
2 What is meant by the term CNC? [2 marks]
3 Give three metal-specific marking-out tools. [3 marks]
4 Use notes and sketches to show how steel would be galvanised. [2 marks]
5 Name a suitable finish for an aluminium sports drinks bottle. [1 mark]

18 Polymers

In the exam you will only need to answer questions on this content in relation to one material category or system. You only need to revise this topic if you plan to answer questions with a focus on polymers.

Selection of materials and components

Polymers have a unique set of properties that open up exciting design and manufacturing opportunities.

Functional needs

- Polymers can easily be moulded to form interesting shapes.
- They are self-coloured and can have a high-gloss finish.
- Polymers are waterproof and chemical-resistant.
- They are good **electrical** and **thermal insulators**.
- Thermosetting polymers are not affected by heat once moulded.

Cost

Financial cost

- Polymers are generally more expensive than timber or metal-based materials.
- However, due to their suitability for quantity production, polymer products can be produced relatively cheaply.

Environmental cost

- Polymers are made from crude oil, which is a non-renewable resource.
- The processing and manufacture of polymer products has a negative effect on the environment.
- Most polymers are recyclable.

Availability

Polymers are widely available in a range of stock forms, including powders and granules.

Figure 18.1 Polymer patio furniture

Electrical insulator: does not conduct electricity.

Thermal insulator: does not conduct heat.

Tolerances

- Polymers lend themselves to being manufactured using sophisticated industrial equipment and can therefore be produced to fine tolerances.
- The laser cutter is an example of a machine that you may have in your school that can cut to very fine tolerances.
- In industry, many polymers are moulded using specific dies. The dies are made to very high tolerances as they will be used to produce thousands of identical components.
- Many of these components must work with other components and therefore must be made to within a specific tolerance. Think of a Lego brick; millions are made and each must fit together with other Lego bricks.

Exam practice answers at www.hoddereducation.co.uk/6 myrevisionnotesdownloads

Material management

Cutting efficiently and minimising waste

- Polymers can be cut using most tools and equipment used to work wood and metal.
- However, there are other methods that can significantly reduce waste and are far more efficient.
- CAD drawings can be manipulated to arrange the components in the most economical way on a given work area.
- This is known as **tessellation**. In industry, special design software will do this automatically.

> **Tessellation**: the arranging of shapes to minimise waste.

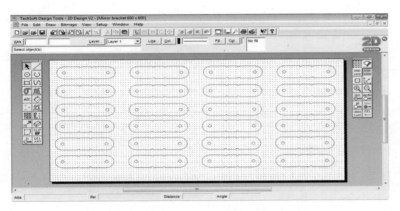

Figure 18.2 A wasteful arrangement of designs

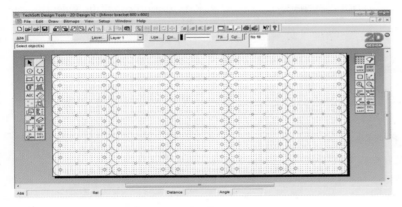

Figure 18.3 Efficient tessellated designs

- A laser cutter is accurate and therefore there is less chance of waste due to human error.
- Very little allowance needs to be given to the width of a laser cut.
- Polymers are suited to moulding. This is a redistribution method of production that produces little waste.

Using appropriate marking-out methods, data points and co-ordinates

- Accurate measuring is essential if a quality prototype is to be manufactured.
- A chinagraph pencil or spirit-based marker is the most effective marking-out tool for use on polymers.

- Paper templates are an efficient way of getting a design onto a polymer surface.
- Templates have the added bonus of providing protection against scratching.
- A laser cutter can be used to etch a design onto sheet polymer.
- A laser cutter uses a datum point or 'home' point from where all measurements are taken.
- The laser will use *x* and *y* co-ordinates to move the laser in two dimensions.

Specialist tools and equipment, techniques and processes

REVISED ☐

There are a wide range of specialist/industrial tools and equipment to use with polymers.

- A laser cutter will etch and cut sheet polymers.
- An injection-moulding machine will inject polymers into a mould.
- A blow-moulding machine will blow air into a preheated polymer tube and enable it to form a hollow shape within a mould.
- A vacuum former will suck a preheated polymer sheet around a mould.
- A 3D printer will layer a preheated filament of polymer to produce a 3D polymer shape.
- Many of these methods involve heating the plastic to a high temperature and therefore it is essential that the correct PPE is worn at all times. For example: wear heatproof gloves when handling hot materials.

Surface treatments and finishes

- **Pigments** are added to polymers at the processing stage to colour the polymer (aesthetics).
- **Stabilisers** may be added to ensure they are not effected by UV light (functional).
- As they are naturally waterproof and chemical-resistant, polymers do not require a protective coating to prevent them from degrading due to weathering or chemicals.

> **Exam tip**
>
> Be able to produce a fully-labelled diagram of an industrial manufacturing process such as injection moulding.

> **Typical mistake**
>
> Candidates will often confuse the injection-moulding machine with the blow-moulding machine.

> **Pigments:** materials added to a polymer to change its colour.
>
> **Stabilisers:** materials added to a polymer to improve its resistance to UV light.

Now test yourself

TESTED ☐

1 Name a suitable polymer for an electric plug socket. [1 mark]
2 Use notes and sketches to describe the process of vacuum forming. [4 marks]
3 What is the function of a stabiliser? [2 marks]

Exam practice answers at **www.hoddereducation.co.uk/6 myrevisionnotesdownloads**

Exam practice

1 Explain how using templates/patterns and jigs increases accuracy in production.
2 State two properties of a timber used to make a child's toy. [2 marks]
3 What do the initials PBS stand for? [1 mark]
4 State two reasons wood is given a finish. [2 marks]
5 Which of the following is a suitable metal for a water tap?
   a) Steel
   b) Aluminium
   c) Lead
   d) Brass [1 mark]
6 Describe what is a meant by a datum point. [1 mark]
7 Explain the process of anodising aluminium. [4 marks]
8 Which of the following is a suitable polymer for a kitchen worktop?
   a) Acrylic (PMMA)
   b) Melamine formaldehyde (MF)
   c) Urea formaldehyde (UF)
   d) High-density polyurethane (HDPE) [1 mark]
9 Use notes and sketches to describe the process of blow moulding a polymer water bottle. [4 marks]
10 How is polymer-based patio furniture protected from the sunlight? [1 mark]

ONLINE

Success in the examination

You will take one written paper that is worth 50 per cent of your total marks. The paper is divided into three sections:

- Section A: Core technical principles (20 marks)
- Section B: Specialist technical principles (30 marks)
- Section C: Designing and making principles (50 marks)

When will the exam be completed?

There is one opportunity to take the exam – in the summer term of your final year.

How long will I have to complete the exam?

- The exam is two hours long and each question has a guide time to help you complete the paper.
- You should practise working past papers and sample questions within the allotted time.

What type of questions will appear in the exam paper?

Section A consists of 20 multiple-choice questions that test your knowledge of the core technical principles.

Here is a typical Section A multiple-choice question.

> **Example**
>
> 1 Which of the following is a composite material:
>   a) Iron
>   b) Teak
>   c) Kevlar
>   d) Cartridge paper

The correct answer is c) Kevlar and for one mark you should indicate it as:

> **Example**
>
> 1 Which of the following is a composite material:
>   a) Iron
>   b) Teak
>   c) Kevlar
>   d) Cartridge paper

Don't answer a multiple-choice question like this:

Example

1 Which of the following is a composite material:
   a) Iron
   b) Teak
   c) Kevlar
   d) Cartridge paper

Exam tip

Never leave a multiple-choice question blank. See if you can eliminate some of the answers you believe to be definitely wrong and then make an educated guess from among the remaining options.

If you mark any more than one box, your answer will not be awarded a mark even if one of your answers is correct.

Section B consists of a mixture of short answer and long answer questions. This section will test your knowledge of specialist technical principles.

This is a typical Section B question:

Example

1 Many products are given a finish to enhance their appearance and give protection. For a material of your choice, name a suitable finish and explain how this finish would be applied.   [4 marks]

Section C consists of a number of short and long answer questions. This section will test your knowledge of design and making principles.

This is a typical Section C question:

Example

Baby's high chair

3 Study the picture of the baby's high chair. Discuss the suitability of the product in terms of its:
   ○ suitability for the user
   ○ aesthetics
   ○ environmental impact.

Tips on preparing for the exam

REVISED ☐

- If you did not understand a topic when it was covered in class, you are unlikely to understand it when revising. Make sure you ask at the end of a lesson if you're unsure of any of the material covered.
- Being absent from school can leave a big hole in your knowledge. Make sure that you catch up any missed work.
- Don't leave revision till the end of the course. Test yourself at the end of each topic.
- Use past papers, online materials and revision guides to help you practise exam-type questions.
- Plan your revision time in the weeks leading up to the exam.
- Make revision cards to help you compartmentalise your understanding.
- Work with other students to test each other.

Approaching the paper

- Make sure you know the date, time and location of your exam.
- Get a good night's sleep. Make sure you have eaten and that you are hydrated.
- Arrive early and make sure you have all your equipment with you.
- Read the instructions on the front cover of the question paper. This will tell you what you have to do.
- Read each question carefully at least twice. This will help you to understand exactly what information you need to give.
- The question will tell you how many marks are available for this question. Use this to gauge how much detail you need to put into your answer.
- The question will tell you how long you should take to answer the question. Use this to help you pace yourself during the exam.
- If you finish early, go back and reread the questions and your answers. You will usually find that you have remembered more detail. You may also be able to spot any mistakes that you may have made.

Sample examination questions

Section A

Example

Which of the following is a modern material?

a) Foam board

b) Metal foam

c) Plywood

d) Stainless steel

Section B

In the exam you will be able to answer Section B questions in relation to **one** chosen material category or system. The sample questions included here each focus on a different material category or system.

Sample question 1: Timber-based materials

Example

Use notes and sketches to describe how you would produce a curve in wood using the industrial process of lamination. [9 marks]

Candidate response

Before you can begin laminating, you need a former that is the same shape as the finished curved piece of wood.

First you need to cut several laminates of wood. These must be thin enough to bend around the former.

A layer of PVA glue is then spread over both sides of the laminates.

Each laminate is then placed into the former.

The former is then clamped together for 24 hours until the glue is dry.

The laminated wood can then be removed and finished by planning and sanding.

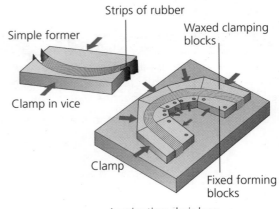

The process of laminating

Assessment comment

This is a complete answer and would be awarded 9 marks. The candidate has provided accurate, labelled sketches that show their understanding of what a former looks like. They have gone on to describe the process of lamination in correctly sequenced, detailed stages using the correct technical terminology.

Mark scheme

Band	Descriptor
7–9	Notes and sketches have been provided to comprehensively describe the process of laminating wood. The stages are correctly sequenced and use the correct technical terminology.
4–6	Notes and sketches have been provided to describe most of the process of laminating wood. The stages are correctly sequenced and some technical terminology has been used.
1–3	Simple notes and/or sketches have been provided to describe some of the process of laminating wood.
0	No response

Sample question 2: Metal-based materials

> **Example**
>
> Explain what is meant by the term alloy. Give an example, properties and uses of an alloy to illustrate your answer.   [6 marks]

Candidate response

An alloy is a combination of two or more metals mixed together to improve their physical and mechanical properties.

Brass is an example of a metal alloy. It is a combination of copper and zinc that produces a strong, ductile metal that is corrosion-resistant and is a good conductor of heat and electricity.

It is used for making water taps and wood screws.

> **Assessment comment**
>
> This is a complete answer that would be awarded 6 marks. A full and correct description of the term alloy has been given, an example of a metal alloy has been provided together with a detail description of its properties and uses.

Mark scheme

Band	Descriptor
5–6	A detailed explanation of the term alloy has been given with a suitable correct example linking its properties to its uses.
3–4	An explanation of the term alloy has been given with a correct example and a suitable use.
1–2	A simple description of the term alloy has been given with a correct example or a correct use.
0	No response

Sample question 3: Polymers

> **Example**
>
> Describe how polymers such as polyethylene (PE) are changed from their primary source into stock form.   [6 marks]

Exam practice answers at **www.hoddereducation.co.uk/6 myrevisionnotesdownloads**

Candidate response

Polyethylene (PE) comes from crude oil that is found underground. It has to be drilled, pumped to the surface and then transported to the refinery by pipe or by tanker.

At the refinery, it is turned into the monomer ethylene by the process of fractional distillation and cracking.

The ethylene monomer is then converted into polyethylene (PE) by a process known as polymerisation.

Polyethylene (PE) is then processed into its stock form by extruding it into a variety of cross sectional shapes.

Assessment comment

This is a complete answer that would be awarded 6 marks. A full explanation of the processing of crude oil into polyethylene (PE) has been given with all the main areas covered.

Mark scheme

Band	Descriptor
5–6	A detailed explanation of the processing of crude oil into polyethylene (PE) has been given with all of the main areas covered.
3–4	An explanation of the processing of crude oil into polyethylene (PE) has been given with most of the main areas covered.
1–2	A brief explanation of the processing of crude oil into polyethylene (PE) given with some areas missing.
0	No response

Section C

Example

Explain how the following are used when designing a product.
- Focus groups
- Ergonomics
- Anthropometric data   [3 x 3 marks]

Candidate response 1

- Focus groups:

Large companies use these to test out their ideas as it involves a group of people giving their opinion through a discussion. This feedback allows for useful primary research to be collected at the initial investigation stages of the design process. It also helps a designer make useful modifications as prototypes can be tested with the focus group too.

- Ergonomics:

Ergonomics is the consideration of how a person interacts with a product. A designer would need to consider this to ensure that the product they design is comfortable and easy to use. Considering aspects such as size, shape, weight and colour make the product more efficient to use.

- Anthropometrics:

Anthropometrics is the size of humans, for example their height, hand span or leg length. This data is used by a designer to ensure that the product they design fits the intended audience. It is common for the 5th to 95th percentile of data to be used, ignoring the extreme sizes. Using anthropometrics ensures that the product is ergonomically designed.

Candidate response 2

- Focus groups:

A type of research where lots of people try out a product

- Ergonomics:

How easy a product is to use

- Anthropometrics:

The size of humans

Mark scheme

For a 3-mark answer the following style of assessment might be used.

Band	Descriptor
3	Three points well made or two points made and justified or two points made and an example given.
2	Two simple points made or a point made and justified or exemplified.
1	A simple point made
0	Nothing worthy of credit

Assessment comment

Candidate One would score 3 marks each time as they give a full explanation of each term and link it back to how a designer might use it to design a product. Detailed statements showing a good understanding.

Candidate Two would score 1 mark for their answers to both ergonomics and anthropometrics as they recall only a simple statement which is a definition of the term. Their answer for focus group may score 2 marks as there is slightly more to their response.

Exam practice answers at **www.hoddereducation.co.uk/6 myrevisionnotesdownloads**

Glossary

Absorbency: how well a material draws up water.

Aesthetics: the style and appearance of a material.

Alignment: when something is in line with something else.

Alloy: a mixture of two or more metals designed to improve the quality of the metal for a given purpose.

Annotation: text and comments added to a diagram to give explanation.

Anodising: a protective oxide layer applied to the surface of aluminium.

Anthropometrics: human dimensions.

Assembly-line production: a series of workers and machines in a factory who progressively assemble identical items.

Automated: a system run completely by machinery through computer control.

Automation: the use of automatic equipment in manufacturing.

Basic blocks: a pattern for each part of a garment that will make a basic garment shape when sewn together.

Batch production: production in which a limited number of the same product is made during a particular period of time.

Bauxite: ore containing aluminium.

Bell-crank linkage: a linkage that changes the direction of the input motion through 90°.

Bespoke: a product that has been specifically made for a client to fulfil their needs.

Biodegradable: something which breaks down and degrades naturally.

Biomimicry: the design of products modelled on nature.

Biopolymers: polymers which are made from plant material such as corn starch.

Blended fabrics: fabrics containing two or more different fibres.

Calendars: rollers which are used in the manufacture of paper to flaten and thin the material.

Cam and follower: a mechanism that converts rotary motion into reciprocating motion when the cam rotates and the follower moves up and down.

Carded: combing staple fibres so that they all lie parallel to each other ready for spinning into a yarn.

Casting: a method of heating metal into a molten state and pouring it into a pre-prepared mould.

Cellulose: fibres which are naturally occurring in plant material.

CNC: computer numerically controlled.

Commercial pattern: ready-made pattern templates used to make textile products.

Composite material: a material that combines the properties of two or more materials.

Computer-aided design (CAD): design work created on computer software packages which can control CAM machines.

Computer-aided manufacture (CAM): manufacture of products using machines which are controlled by computers.

Computer numerically controlled (CNC): automated machines which are operated by computers.

Concave: a surface that curves inwards.

Conductive fabrics: textiles that conduct electricity.

Contamination: exposure to a polluting substance.

Contemporary: present-day design.

Converging: meeting at a point.

Conversion: (of timber) the process of cutting a log up into planks.

Co-operative: a business owned, governed and self-managed by its workers.

Crating: a series of faint lines which help to build the final sketch.

Crease: make a shallow indent in the material so that it can be folded easily.

Cross filing: a method of shaping metal using files.

Crowdfunding: a method of funding a project by raising money from large numbers of people using the internet.

Cubist: early 20th-century design, making use of geometry and interlocking planes.

Culture: the values, beliefs, customs and behaviours of groups of people and societies.

Datum point: a known starting point; a point of reference from which further measurements can be made.

Depth-stop: a mechanical means of setting the depth that a drill bit will cut, used for quality control.

Die cutter: shapes can be punched or stamped out cleanly.

Draw filing: a method of smoothing the edges of metal.

Dyeing: the permanent application of colour to a fibre or fabric to give a uniform colour.

Effort: an input force applied to move an object.

Electrical insulator: something which does not conduct electricity.

Engrave: carve or etch onto the surface of an object.

Ergonomics: human interaction with products.

E-textiles: textiles that use smart materials.

Ethics: moral principles.

Evolve: to develop gradually.

Exploitation: the action or fact of treating someone unfairly in order to benefit from their work.

Extrusion: an industrial process involving heating polymer granules and forcing them through a die to produce long, uniform, cross-sectional polymer products.

Fabric selvedge: the finished edge of the fabric where the weft turns around the warp during weaving to leave an edge that does not fray.

Face side and face edge: two adjacent surfaces of wood that have been planed flat and square.

Fair trade: a movement that aims to achieve fair and better trading conditions and opportunities that promote sustainability for developing countries.

Felling: the process of cutting down trees.

Ferrous metals: metals that contain iron, are magnetic but are prone to rusting.

Finite resource: a resource that will run out.

First-order lever: a lever that has the fulcrum anywhere between the effort and the load.

Fission: division or splitting of an atom.

Flexible manufacturing system (FMS): flexibility in a system which allows it to react to predicted or unpredicted changes during manufacturing.

Flow soldering: an industrial method of soldering where a solder paste is melted by heating a PCB.

Focus group: a large group of people who feed back their opinions.

Forest Stewardship Council (FSC): an organisation which helps to manage trees and avoid deforestation.

Fossil fuels: coal, oil and gas which are finite resources and are found naturally.

Fractional distillation: the process of separating crude oil into its different parts.

Friction: the resistance to movement when two surfaces rub together.

Functional: an object which works well and fulfils its purpose or job.

Functionality: how well an object or a material will fit its intended purpose.

Galvanising: a protective coating of zinc applied to the surface of steel.

Gear train: a mechanism with two wheels with teeth around the edge that interlock and transmit rotary motion and torque; a line of meshing gears.

Generator: a machine for converting mechanical energy into electricity.

Geometric: use of shapes and angles in design.

Global warming: an increase in the temperature of the Earth's atmosphere due to higher levels of CO_2.

Go-no-go gauge: a special tool that checks the size of a metal component.

Greenhouse effect: the effect of pollution in the atmosphere causing the sun's heat to get trapped in the lower atmosphere and warm up the planet.

Green timber: timber that has just been felled and contains a lot of moisture.

Haematite: ore containing iron.

Hardwoods: woods which come from deciduous trees and are generally hard and durable.

Human factors: issues relating to people.

Iconic: product which is held in high regard, is well known, has influenced others or withstood the test of time.

Ingeo™: a high-performance biodegradable fibre made from corn starch.

Ingots: bars of metal that can be processed.

Injection moulding: an industrial process where polymer granules are heated and injected into a mould.

Innovation: inventing and developing ideas into products.

Innovative: advanced or original.

Input device: an electrical or mechanical sensor that uses signals from the environment and converts them into signals that can be passed to processing devices and components.

Integrated circuit (IC): a self-contained circuit made up of separate components that act as process devices in an electronic system; a miniature electronic circuit on a semi-conductor.

Interfacing: a woven or non-woven fabric used as an extra layer to give additional strength and help to keep the shape of a textile product.

Intricate: design which is complex.

Jig: a three-dimensional aid to a production process.

Exam practice answers at **www.hoddereducation.co.uk/6 myrevisionnotesdownloads**

Just in time (JIT) production: an approach to production which reduces flow time as items needed are delivered just in time for the assembly of the product.

KD (knock-down) fittings: commercially-made fittings generally used with self-assembly furniture.

Lean manufacturing: focusing on reduction of waste when manufacturing.

Lever: a simple mechanism that changes an input motion and force into an output motion and force.

Life cycle assessment: understanding the impact a product has, from the extraction of its raw materials to its disposal at the end of its useful lifespan.

Light-dependent resistor (LDR): an input device used to detect light levels, in which resistance increases in low light and decreases in intense light.

Light-emitting diode (LED): an output device that produces light.

Linear motion: movement in a straight line.

Linkage: a mechanism that transfers force and changes the direction of movement.

Load: an output force.

Manipulated: changed and controlled to fit the design.

Manufactured boards: man-made boards that come in large sizes and are usually flat and stable.

Market pull: where users want an existing product to be improved or redeveloped to meet their needs.

Mass production: manufacturing in large quantities over a long period of time.

Mechanism: a device that changes an input motion into an output motion.

Microcontroller: a small computer with a single integrated circuit used to provide functionality and control.

Microencapsulated: Fibres with nano-sized chemical capsules in the fibre structure. Rubbing activates the capsules which release their contents.

Microfibres: very fine fibres – 60 times finer than human hair – made from polyamide or polyester.

Milling: the machining of material to produce grooves, slots and flat surfaces.

Modern material: a material that has recently been developed.

Monomers: the individual building blocks used to create polymers.

Nap: a one-directional raised or brushed surface.

Natural fibres: fibres from plant and animal sources.

Nested: also known as tessellated; fitting as many shapes as possible next to one another on a sheet of material, with minimal space in between, in order to avoid waste.

Non-ferrous metals: metals that do not contain iron and therefore do not rust.

Non-finite resource: a resource that if managed properly will not run out.

Non-woven fabrics: fabrics made directly from fibres without the need to make them into yarns first.

Obsolete: something which is no longer useful or which is out of date.

One-off manufacture: manufacture in which only one complete product is made.

One-way pattern: a fabric design that has one direction.

Opacity: the density of a material and whether light can be seen through it.

Ore: rock which contains metal.

Organic cotton: cotton grown with fewer chemical pesticides and fertilisers than standard cotton.

Orthographic: a 2D working drawing which shows the views and dimensions of a product so that a third party can manufacture it.

Ornate: highly decorative.

Oscillating motion: movement swinging from side to side.

Output device: a device that sends out information to the environment.

Patent: a form of intellectual property which protects a designer's ideas.

Patterns: a marking-out aid which ensures exact copies of a shape or part can be made.

Perforate: to make a series of cuts in a form of a dotted line.

Perspective: the height, width and depth of an object drawn in relation to each other.

Photochromic: a material that reacts to light.

Pick and place machine: an industrial machine used to surface mount electronic components onto the surface of a PCB.

Pigments: materials added to a polymer to change its colour.

Pivot or fulcrum: a fixed point around which a mechanism moves.

Planed all round (PAR): timber that has all sides planed; also known as 'planed square edge (PSE)'.

Planed both sides (PBS): timber that has had two sides planed.

Planed square edge (PSE): timber that has all sides planed; also know as 'planed all round (PAR)'.

Plying: twisting two or more single yarns together to make a multi-ply yarn.

Polymerisation: joining monomers together to form polymers.

Pop art: art based on modern popular culture.

Postmodernistic: designs which consider the aesthetics of an object more than its functionality.

Potatopak: packaging material made from starch.

Precious metal: a rare metal that is expensive, such as gold.

Press forming: the process of softening a thermoforming polymer and pressing it into a mould.

Primary research: investigations carried out first hand.

Printed circuit board (PCB): a board that supports and connects electronic components.

Process device: a device that handles information received from an input device and turn outputs on and/or off.

Profit margin: financial gain between what has been spent and what has been earned.

Programmable interface controller (PIC): a programmable integrated circuit.

Proportion: sizes in relation to one another.

Prototype: a first or initial version of a product; an early sample, model, or release of a product, made to test a concept or a process.

Pulleys and belts: a mechanism of two small wheels connected by a belt that transmit rotary motion.

Push/pull or parallel-motion linkage: a linkage in which the direction of motion and the magnitude of the forces are the same.

Quality control: checks made during manufacture to ensure accuracy is maintained.

Raw material: material before it has undergone processing; the state a material is first found in (for example, ores from the ground before they are processed into metals).

Recessed: set back into the surface.

Reciprocating motion: movement backwards and forwards in a straight line.

Recycled: material which has had another use or purpose previously and has been reprocessed and made into a new product.

Refining: the processing of crude oil.

Regenerated fibres: fibres made by chemically modifying cellulose from spruce trees or cotton linters.

Rendering: adding colour to a drawing to enhance communication.

Renewable: a source of material or energy which, if managed responsibly, will not run out.

Robotics: technology involved in the design, building, operation and use of robots.

Rotary motion: movement round in a circle.

Rough sawn: timber straight from the saw.

Scale drawing: a drawing with accurate relative sizes that have been enlarged or reduced by a certain amount.

Scoring: lightly cutting the surface of a material so that it folds cleanly.

Seasoning: the process of removing moisture from newly-converted planks.

Secondary research: using the investigations of others.

Second-order lever: a lever that has the load and effort on the same side of the fulcrum.

Semi-precious metal: metal such as copper, that is more expensive than common metals such as steel.

Serrated: a blade that has ridges in it to allow it to perforate a material.

Shape memory alloy (SMA): a metal that will return to its original shape when placed in hot water.

Smart material: a material that reacts to environmental changes such as heat and light.

Smelting: the process of extracting metal from ore.

Softwoods: woods which come from coniferous trees that are relatively fast growing.

Spinning: twisting fibres together to make a yarn.

Stabilisers: materials added to a polymer to improve its resistance to UV light.

Standard components: mass produced parts that are all identical and can be used and replaced in many products easily.

Standardised: in which all parts are the same and identical so can be replaced easily.

Standardised sizes: a set of body measurements that conform to the British Standards Institute (BSI) standard sizing.

Stock size: standard form of materials for purchase and manufacture.

Sub-assembly: a separate manufacturing line that makes small sections of a product, such as collars, ready to add to the final product being made.

Summative: assessing the whole process after completion.

Sustainability: design which considers environmental impacts, both in the long and short term; designing to maintain the environment today and in the future.

Switch: an input device that senses when pressure is applied.

Synthetic fibres: fibres manufactured from oil-based chemicals.

System: a set of parts or components that work together and provide functionality to products and processes.

Tanilising: a method of pressure-treating wood with a preservative.

Task analysis: looking at the design task or brief in depth and asking questions.

Technical textiles: textiles manufactured for their functional capabilities.

Technology push: where new technologies or materials are developed and designers develop new products that use them.

Template: a pattern shape, usually made from paper or card, used to cut out fabric to the size and shape required; a two-dimensional profile of an object that is to be cut.

Tessellation: the arranging of shapes to minimise waste.

Thermal insulator: material which does not conduct heat.

Thermistor: an input device in which resistance changes with changes in temperature.

Thermochromatic: a material that reacts to heat.

Thermoforming polymers: polymers that can be formed and shaped with the use of heat.

Thermoplastic fibres: these soften when heated and can be heat-set into new shapes.

Thermosetting polymers: polymers that once formed cannot be reformed with the use of heat.

Third-order lever: a lever that has the load and effort on the same side of the fulcrum, but the load is further away from the fulcrum and therefore the effort needed is greater than the load.

Tolerance: the acceptable difference between the upper and lower given sizes; the allowable amount of variation of a specified dimension within which quality will still be assured.

Tolerance level: the acceptable variation in the size a product or part of a product, usually given as an upper and a lower limit.

Tone: the deepness or brightness of a shade of colour.

Torque: a turning force that causes rotation.

Triangulation: use of triangles in structures to increase strength.

Turbine: a wheel inside a machine which is rotated by a flow of water or other fluid, or steam or gas.

Turning: a method of producing cylinders and cones using a centre lathe.

Vacuum forming: a process that involves heating a thermoforming polymer and sucking it around a mould.

Virtual marketing: marketing techniques that get websites, social networks or their users to pass on marketing messages to other websites and users to increase brand awareness.

Virtual model: a model produced using CAD software to understand the product without actually making it.

Virtual retailing: selling products on the internet.